Corporate Realities and Environmental Truths

Corporate Realities and Environmental Truths

Strategies for Leading Your Business in the Environmental Era

Steven J. Bennett
Richard Freierman
Stephen George

John Wiley & Sons, Inc.
New York • Chichester • Brisbane • Toronto • Singapore

Library of Congress Cataloging-in-Publication Data

Bennett, Steven J., 1951–
    Corporate realities and environmental truths : strategies for leading your business
in the environmental era / Steven J. Bennett, Stephen George, Richard Freierman.
     p.   cm.
   Includes index.
   ISBN 0-471-53073-5 (alk. paper)
    1. Pollution—Economic aspects—United States. 2. Strategic planning—
Environmental aspects—United States. 3. United States—Industries—
Environmental aspects. 4. Green marketing—United States. 5. Green movement—
United States—Case studies. I. George, Stephen, 1948–
II. Freierman, Richard. III. Title.
HD69.P6B46   1993
658.4'08—dc20   93-3481

Printed in the United States of America

10 9 8 7 6 5 4 3 2 1

Acknowledgments

Many people contributed to our understanding of the complex relationship between business, economics, and the environment. In particular, we'd like to thank Cameron Beers of The Gillette Company; Barbara Baklarz and Rich Larris of AT&T; Elaine Matthews of Procter & Gamble; Alison Silverstein of Pacific Gas & Electric; Glenda Goehrs of GSD&M; and Peter Kinder of Kinder, Lydenberg, Domini & Company.

We'd also like to thank our editor, John Mahaney, for his patience, support, and help in sharing the project. Gloria Fuzia helped with a number of administrative details—thanks!

Contents

vii

INTRODUCTION

THE GREENING OF AMERICAN BUSINESS
Becoming a Winner in the Environmental Marketplace

REACH OUT AND TOUCH SOMEONE

On the morning of May 18, 1990, James Ben Messenger, systems administrator for the Commonwealth of Massachusetts's Division of Insurance, looked up with curiosity when the mail clerk dropped off a parcel roughly the size of two phone books and bearing AT&T's logo. The only item he'd ordered recently from AT&T was a set of small cardboard inserts for the 24 telephones in his division; the inserts, which display the number of the primary line connected to the phone, had vanished through years of office changes and desk shuffling. To his amazement, the box *did* contain the inserts he'd ordered from the AT&T catalog. But the shipper had

1

stuffed them in an envelope nestled in a dense bed of polystyrene peanuts. Messenger thought wryly that using that much packaging to cushion cardboard was akin to driving the space shuttle *Discovery* to the corner store to pick up a carton of milk.

But his amusement quickly turned to anger as he contemplated the polystyrene explosion that had hit his desk. Brushing off the peanuts sticking to his phone, he worked through directory assistance until he found the number for AT&T's New Jersey headquarters. A bit of digging and patience put him in touch with AT&T's Senior Staff Engineer in charge of special environmental projects, Walter Boyhan. Boyhan listened quietly and took notes as Messenger unfolded his complaint and then concluded the conversation by asking for the name of someone to whom he should write to complain formally about such an unsound packaging practice. "My boss," answered Boyhan, "David Chittick, VP of Environment and Safety Engineering." Messenger confirmed the spelling, then dashed off the following letter:

Dear Mr. Chittick,

I recently ordered and received inserts for our phones here at the Division of Insurance (Item #846239846). I was astounded and dismayed when they arrived because they were packed in a 5"h × 9½"w × 12"l box *filled* with "PELASPAN-PAC" loose-fill. I am amazed that in this day and age, a customer-oriented company like yours is shipping their products in such a wasteful and environmentally irresponsible manner. I would assume that shipping such an order as ours (25 phone inserts) in an appropriate size envelope would be less expensive for you in terms of packing materials, labor, and shipping costs, and would obviously not add near the amount of waste to our already overflowing landfills.

It seems to me that your organization can become more cost-efficient and environmentally responsible by adopting simple, but effective ideas such as the one that I have suggested.

Please consider alternative packaging techniques in the future.

After sealing the letter and popping it in the outbound mail box, Messenger felt better; at least he had given voice to his innate New England sense of thrift, not to mention his sentiments as an environmentalist. The last thing he expected was any kind of formal response to his letter or phone call, much less the following reply from Mr. Chittick, dated July 17, 1990:

Dear Mr. Messenger,

Confirming your recent telephone conversation with Mr. Boyhan of my organization, we want to thank you for bringing to our attention a wasteful packaging practice associated with a recent purchase you made from our AT&T Catalog. I can assure you that we are chagrined and share your dismay at our use of inappropriate packaging.

We have contacted the engineering staff for our Material Distribution Centers (MDCs) and the Methods Supervisor, and have received their assurances that more efficient packaging practices will be instituted as rapidly as possible. By way of explanation, let me point out that current practices were undoubtedly designed to minimize overall costs at each MDC by standardizing a limited number of cartons for all products to be shipped from that center. Apparently, no one anticipated that anything small enough to be slipped into an envelope would be ordered. We have instituted an examination of company-wide packaging procedures in an effort to reduce the overall cost of packaging and to take into account its impact on the environment when the customer disposes of it.

Again, let me thank you for bringing this matter to our attention. If you should observe other practices that seem to be inefficient, please contact me or Mr. Boyhan.

THE WAVE OF THE FUTURE

More remarkable than a letter from such a high-ranking corporate official for such a seemingly trivial problem was the investigation that AT&T launched upon receiving Messenger's complaint. The inquiry, led by Walter Boyhan, started in New Jersey and, over the course of two months, made its way down the eastern seaboard and across the Gulf states until it finally ended at a small outside contractor's operation in Missouri. The contractor had never fulfilled any catalog orders in anything smaller than the 5"h × 9½"w × 12"l box and had therefore followed the same routine with Mr. Messenger's cardboard inserts.

AT&T's investigation proved to be an opportunity for Boyhan to explore virtually all of the company's packaging procedures. Along the line, Boyhan's office issued numerous bulletins with new packaging guidelines for each area within the corporation. And although we cannot precisely measure the impact of the bulletins on costs and the quality of the environment, we can learn several important lessons from the Messenger incident.

First, the story highlights the fact that every decision and move in a company, regardless of scope, makes its mark on the environment. Decisions and practices in the purchasing and shipping departments can have just as much impact on the environment as decisions made in the engineering and manufacturing divisions. And although no one deliberately sets out to cause pollution, use unnecessary packaging, or design products that can't be disposed of responsibly or safely, few employees, managers, or executives know how to include crucial environmental concerns in their everyday thinking. It is therefore vitally important to open people's eyes and minds and get them thinking in terms of the "environmental bottom line."

Second, it is the cumulative result of environmental actions—positive and negative—that makes a difference. A product or packaging design that doesn't account for ultimate disposal may not seem like a major issue when you consider a single unit. But a year's worth of production that creates tens of millions of units could have a significant impact on limited landfill space. Just look at disposable diapers. Heralded as an ingenious breakthrough in the late seventies, who would have thought that they would become the environmental scourge of the late eighties?

Likewise, an unnecessary shipping practice, like the case of the AT&T phone inserts, might only infuriate a handful of customers, but hundreds of thousands of instances that go unnoticed will amount to additional burdens on scarce landfill space.

The flip side of the coin is that the cure for many environmental ills also starts with small, discrete steps that do not require massive injections of cash and technology. Of course, abating global problems like acid rain or cleaning up hazardous waste sites does require significant amounts of money, sophisticated technology, and expertise. But for other problems, the real cure starts with simple initiatives at the grassroots level, perhaps inspired by company programs that boost employees' and managers' awareness of the environmental consequences of everyday decisions and provide them with the tools they need to make their work more environmentally responsible.

Take a simple action like maintaining the tire pressure in company cars and trucks—underinflated tires can rob the vehicle of 5 percent of its mileage. On a cumulative scale, that amounts to a tremendous waste of gasoline and money and increased air pollution.

Or consider how people in a company use paper. Most are accustomed to using one side only and then discarding it. They're also accustomed to making needless photocopies and generating copies of reports that are tossed out without even being read. By getting employees to think about paper as a precious resource, one whose manufacture and disposal creates various types of pollution, companies can spare the environment, cut back on waste, and save a substantial amount of money.

This line of thinking applies even to heavy manufacturing processes. Every minute, thousands of gallons of solvent and treatment wash are wasted. As many companies are discovering, tremendous quantities can be reclaimed through available technology or simply not used at all—if your people are thinking in terms of reuse, recycling, and source reduction.

The point is, if your employees are given a mandate to look upon their jobs from an ecological perspective, they'll find ways to cut waste and curb pollution; they will no more think of shipping off cardboard inserts in an absurdly unnecessary package than they would empty trash cans out the window. And when forced into environmentally irresponsible behaviors beyond their control, they'll demand alternatives from their managers and supervisors. The real moral of the AT&T phone insert story is this: When employees operate on autopilot, they'll be oblivious to their impact on the environment. But when they understand the environmental implications of their work, they can take dramatic actions that benefit both the environment and the company's bottom line.

BALANCING CORPORATE REALITIES AND ENVIRONMENTAL TRUTHS

Today, companies have the option of developing their own approaches to solving environmental problems. Tomorrow, most won't; the scope of our environmental problems will force legislators into taking actions that may have severe repercussions for businesses. And although lobbying groups have succeeded in making some environmental legislation more palatable, everyone in business should be aware of the inevitable tough regulations that will be enacted to curb problems such as severe air pollution, acid rain, ozone depletion, global warming, and a scarcity of acceptable landfill space. These environmental truths will increasingly affect your bottom line. Not only will it cost you to comply with environmental regulations, but increasingly activist consumers, concerned with saving the environment and convinced that corporations are responsible for most environmental ills, will also cast their vote in the checkout lines of the nation's stores.

At the same time that the world is looking at your business for signs of environmental responsibility, you have a financial responsibility to your shareholders; after all, you're in business to make a profit, grow, and compete effectively. These are your corporate realities—and they sometimes conflict with environmental realities.

A GUIDE FOR THE PERPLEXED

Corporate Realities and Environmental Truths is a blueprint for successful environmental action. It identifies opportunities and pitfalls and shows you how to maximize your resources in the environmental arena. In Chapter 1 you'll learn five prerequisites to managing a more environmentally responsible company. With these in place, you can implement a Total Quality Environmental Management (TQEM) program (see Chapter 2) that will enable you to achieve environmental goals while improving your company's internal communication and empowering your employees to make effective decisions. In Chapter 3, you'll learn how to develop a environmental management structure appropriate for your type of business and culture and how to harness the grass-roots energy of your employees. Chapter 4 continues the grass-roots theme and describes how to create an "organic office" that provides people with an environmentally fit workplace—you can only ask people to care about the environment at large if you provide the wherewithal to manage the day-to-day environment in which they carry out their jobs.

Chapter 5 offers ten "laws" of environmental marketing that will help you frame your message in a way that has the best chance of meeting public approval and avoiding problems with state and federal lawmakers. Chapter 6 probes the effective use of environmental communications—how to structure a PR campaign that conveys your goals and achievements and initiates a dialogue with the public.

In Chapter 7, you'll learn how to form partnerships with community groups and environmental organizations—a joining of forces that just several years ago was unheard of. Through environmental partnerships, you'll involve your stakeholders and outside experts in solving environmental problems. And in working side by side in the spirit of cooperation, you'll break down the walls that have traditionally led to adversarial relationships between the business and environmental communities.

Chapter 8 outlines the kind of proactive approaches that businesses can use to become vanguard environmental companies. By adopting the strategies discussed in this chapter, you'll also learn how to take preemptive actions that will boost your image with the public and activist organizations and to ward off the need for potentially costly regulation.

Chapter 9 reveals how public watchdog and social responsibility groups evaluate the environmental performance of companies. You'll learn how your company may be viewed by what are becoming increasingly vocal and influential forces in U.S. business.

Finally, the Epilogue defines the major environmental challenges that all businesses will face in the twenty-first century.

We hope that the principles and case studies provided in *Corporate Realties and Environmental Truths* will not only help you avoid the kind of mistakes that tarnish company names and reputations but will also enable you to proceed down a clear path leading to a cleaner environment and a healthier bottom line.

CHAPTER 1

FIVE PREREQUISITES FOR CORPORATE ENVIRONMENTAL ACTION
Meeting the Environmental Imperative

"If 90 percent of your customers paid you to package 'green,' wouldn't you be awfully stupid not to?" Malcolm Forbes asked this question of his readers in 1989. This proclamation, by the self-acclaimed "quintessential capitalist tool," characterized the business world's excitement over the discovery of the "green consumer." But in less than three years, the discovery that people would consider environmental quality in their purchasing decisions has been eclipsed by a growing awareness of the broad environmental responsibilities that all businesses today must shoulder.

Not only are consumers demanding more environmentally responsible goods and services, but companies will also have to navigate through an increasingly complex web of laws in

11

the years to come. And although it is unlikely that regulations with the sweeping scope of the Resource Conservation Recovery Act or the Toxic Substances Control Act will be promulgated in the near future, individual states are likely to pass regulations that could have dramatic national impact.

Just look at California's Proposition 65, passed in 1990, which requires manufacturers to place warning labels on products that contain any of 475 chemicals known to cause cancer or birth defects. Faced with the choice of developing special (and potentially frightening) labeling just for the California market, some companies chose to simply eliminate the offending agents. Other states are passing laws regarding environmental claims in labeling and advertising. And still others are considering legislation that could force companies to radically alter their product formulations, labeling, and packaging.

Another type of pressure will come from employees who demand more environmentally responsible workplaces; today's workers expect their companies to reduce waste and pollution and to minimize their exposure to environmental hazards. They're better informed than any previous generation of workers. And many who have begun to adopt ecologically friendly practices at home, such as recycling, conserving energy, and purchasing environmentally sound products, want their companies to follow suit. Smart companies will provide the means for enabling people to achieve their conservationist goals; this will not only boost job satisfaction but could also result in substantial cost reductions as well. And in the near future, to attract the best and brightest talent, companies will have to demonstrate a shiny environmental track record and an ongoing commitment to preserving the balance of nature—tomorrow's graduates, who grew up with trips to community recycling centers in the family station wagon, will not tolerate excuses.

Finally, concern for the environment has mobilized the most well-informed and powerful watchdog groups in the history of business. No company can afford to ignore or merely pay lip service to organizations such as the Council on Economic Priorities, which grades companies according to their performance on social and environmental issues and then publishes its results in *Shopping for a Better World*—which now has nearly 9 million copies in print.

Similarly, ethical or socially responsible investing is having a major impact in the financial world; the Social Investment Forum estimates that more than $650 billion is currently invested in "screened vehicles" (investment products that are selected on the basis of ethical, environmental, and political criteria). And Peter Kinder, of Kinder, Lydenberg, and Domini, a leading research firm in the ethical investment field, believes that the number is actually much higher: "We run into many investment houses that have been using screens for years at a client's request—they simply never labeled it as 'ethical investing.' If you could total up all the firms that are using screened vehicles, the total amount invested would probably exceed a trillion dollars—that's quite staggering when you consider that the entire commercial paper market is $530 billion."

In short, every company today faces a number of highly compelling reasons to "go green." But doing so entails more than talk, meetings, and tidings of green cheer from the CEO; to succeed with environmental issues, a company must exhibit "buy-in" from top leaders, develop an understanding of the role that people play in causing and preventing environmental problems, integrate environmental issues into its strategic planning process, and display a willingness both to exceed compliance levels and to work with its stakeholders outside the company. The rest of this chapter is devoted to each of these topics.

TAKE EXECUTIVE ACTION

To succeed with environmental issues, top management, especially the president or CEO, must maintain high visibility and demonstrate a personal commitment to the program. Consider the situation at DuPont. Since 1984, part of Corporate Environmental Officer Bruce Karrh's job involved advising the plant managers about their expenditures for environmental projects. Karrh often met with resistance—until Edward Woolard, Jr., DuPont's chairman, called for "corporate environmentalism." With the explicit backing of the CEO, Karrh no longer had to work to convince the plant managers of the importance of this issue—suddenly, they were calling *him* to ask for assistance.

The fact is, the entire company responds to the environmental imperative when the CEO and/or president demonstrates support and commitment; a strong signal from the executive offices sends ripples throughout the entire company, whether the issue in question be recycling programs, pollution control, or health considerations.

In addition to making a long-term commitment to the environment through policy statements, speeches, and endorsing corporate programs, senior executives can take a number of actions to ensure that the company will make meaningful improvements in this area.

Personal encouragement in the form of memos and speeches at company meetings are effective means for top executives to demonstrate involvement with environmental issues. Another is to meet informally with the people on the front lines and get a firsthand sense of what they're doing to achieve their companies' goals. That kind of personal interest will not only motivate the people who are making the program happen but can also send a strong message to those who haven't "signed up" yet.

For example, when Colman M. Mockler, Jr., the late chairman of Gillete, was leaving Boston for a trip to England, he asked Cameron Beers, director of administrative services, if he could do anything to help the company's environmental and energy programs in the United Kingdom. Beers then described one facility where a very enthusiastic plant manager was not receiving support from his managing director, and he asked Mockler to "look into the situation." When Mockler arrived at Gillette's London plant, he paid a visit to the managing director, asking him to pass along his personal thanks to the plant manager for the excellent job he'd been doing on the environmental front. The message was well received.

Then there's the case of the AT&T recycling reminder cards. When the leaders of AT&T's recycling team undertook an enforcement program to improve compliance (some people were simply throwing their office paper into the regular trash cans), they proposed placing cards on the desks of offenders to remind them of the recycling program's guidelines. Because of the potential for embarrassment on the part of the recipients—as well as the discomfort of the cleaning staff charged with putting them on the desks of potentially senior people—the team leaders sought the support of top management.

Recycling was only one of the environmental issues that CEO Robert Allen faced at the time. His response was to issue the "AT&T Policy for Environmental Protection," which laid out a comprehensive plan for the company. With Allen's support behind the program, the recycling team leaders had all the clout they needed to proceed with their plans for using the reminder cards. In addition, they implemented a follow-up procedure: If the reminder is not heeded after one card is left, the cleaning staff will not empty that person's trash receptacles. Had Allen not issued the policy, chances are that the cards may have been ignored or become the source of

15

internal wrangling. Given the scope of environmental problems, the recycling cards may seem insignificant, but they've helped make AT&T's recycling program one of the most successful in the country.

RECOGNIZE THE PEOPLE FACTOR

Traditionally, top managers have considered environmental problems to be technical or engineering issues—if there's a pollution problem, just "let the boys from engineering or maintenance get down there with their screwdrivers and wrenches. . . . they'll take of it."

But according to environmental management consultant Suzanne Gauntlett, the times are changing, and executives must stop thinking of the environment in purely technical and regulatory terms: "We've tended to think of the environment in terms of an end-of-the-pipe philosophy that equates pollution control with placing a piece of equipment at the end of the manufacturing process. Likewise, regulatory compliance has been thought of as a matter of better scrubbers, better filters, and more paperwork. Unfortunately, this mindset overlooks a critical component: the human factor. Look at the three worst environmental disasters of the past decade: Bhopal, Chernobyl, and Valdez. Human error was responsible in all three cases—the people involved simply failed to follow the correct policies and procedures. Better technologies in themselves do not motivate people to perform their jobs properly or make the right decisions."

As Gauntlett points out, top executives must understand that environmental action begins and ends with people, whether the issue is pollution prevention, recycling, or solid waste reduction. And motivation is the key issue; if people

16

believe that their job description includes helping the company perform in an environmentally responsible fashion, then dramatic improvements will follow.

Again, role modeling is critical. If top executives stress the fact that environmental solutions rest on people, not technologies, then other managers will likely adopt a similar attitude. That trickle-down effect will continue until those at the line level understand that people create pollution and therefore only people can prevent it.

Finally, thinking of your people as problem solvers is critical to paving the way for a total environmental quality management program (see Chapter 2). If employees feel like they "check their brains at the door" when they go to work, then they'll treat environmental problems as they do any others. For continuous improvement to work, everyone—from the boiler room to the boardroom—must be regarded as an expert problem solver in his or her own area.

INCLUDE ENVIRONMENTAL ISSUES IN THE STRATEGIC PLANNING PROCESS

In a 1991 address to Yale University, 3M Company's Robert P. Bringer, staff vice-president, environmental engineering and pollution control, stated that "business interests have now merged with environmental interests. Forward-looking companies are now building the environmental issue into their strategies. Forward-looking companies are starting now to make investments in research and development which will make their facilities and products more environmentally sound. Many of the research objectives necessary to achieve this goal will also lead to lower costs, higher quality, more marketable products, fewer liabilities, better employee morale, and enhanced corporate reputation. Companies who do not include the environmental issue in their strategy risk losing their competitive position in the long run."

Bringer's own company melds environmental concerns with strategic initiatives, as demonstrated by its program to reclaim plastic foam packaging materials from its bulk videotape customers. This lowers disposal costs for 3M's customers—something that Japanese and Korean competitors cannot do—and at the same time saves 3M money because it can reuse the packaging. The result of this clever maneuver is a competitive advantage for 3M and a reduction in non-recyclable waste that would otherwise wind up in landfills or incinerators.

Procter & Gamble also incorporated environmental issues into its strategic planning when it chose to offer its Downy fabric softener in a refillable package in 1989. Consumers were able to purchase one 64-ounce plastic container, use the contents, and then buy a concentrated refill pouch to empty into the original containers. The pouches required 75 percent less packaging material, giving the company an impressive cost advantage that translated into the opportunity to compete on the basis of price. It also positioned the company more favorably with environmentally conscious consumers. In 1993, Procter & Gamble introduced Ultra Downy, which, in addition to continuing the refill concept, added the benefit of original packaging from 100 percent post-consumer recycled plastic.

Pacific Gas & Electric has launched major programs in conservation, alternative energy generation, and natural resource stewardship. Back in the mid-1970s, when the company announced plans for major power plant expansions, it met with fierce resistance from organizations like the Environmental Defense Fund. As a result of its environmental programs, the company is now regarded as one of the nation's leaders in the electric industry.

Finally, Xerox Corporation has long understood the importance of factoring environmental issues into the early stages of product design. Since 1965, the company has been reclaiming photoreceptor materials from large volume copiers and has recently instituted a program for reclaiming customer-replaceable cartridges.

According to Abhay Bhushan, Xerox's manager of environmental leadership programs, Xerox has a "strong quality process and customer orientation and an emphasis on teamwork. By addressing environmental issues within this framework, we can simultaneously improve return on assets, market share, and most importantly, customer satisfaction. . . . Many Xerox customers want to recycle to eliminate waste. Providing them with options to recycle copy cartridges and office waste paper directly increases their satisfaction with our products."

STRIVE TO EXCEED COMPLIANCE LEVELS

Companies on the environmental cutting edge often establish goals that take them beyond simply abiding by government regulations. To accomplish these goals, they develop comprehensive means for measuring the environmental performance of the corporation as a whole, its individual divisions, and its managers. This also positions them for a successful total quality environmental management (TQEM) program; TQEM depends on realistic assessments as well as the relentless drive for continuous improvement. By raising the high bar above mere compliance, you prepare your company for ongoing improvement and change for the better.

Kodak, for example, has a structured worldwide site assessment program designed to keep the company in compliance with regulations and, at the same time, identify opportunities to exceed government requirements. Part of the criteria used in site audits is derived from the explicit goals set forth by the company's Management Committee on Environmental Responsibility. Kodak also includes environmental objectives in the operating plan. As such, these objectives are a factor in evaluating the performance of middle and upper management for some divisions, where they are among the important criteria upon which salary review is based.

To improve their internal environmental auditing procedures, some companies, such as Chevron Corporation, are turning to outside consultants to "audit the auditors." In retaining AD Little of Cambridge, Massachusetts to review its internal procedures, Chevron acknowledged that auditing is the principal measure of its environmental performance. Although programs such as these have not yet reached the stringency of financial audits, they ensure that the policies established by top management are indeed put into practice. This, in turn, can only enhance the credibility of the company in the eyes of its employees and critics.

Companies on the environmentalist vanguard go beyond compliance with environmental regulations; they exceed the regulations whenever possible. AT&T, for example, announced that by mid-May 1993 it would eliminate virtually all ozone-depleting substances from its consumer and business products manufacturing operations. This goal is considerably more aggressive than the terms set forth in the Montreal Protocol, an international treaty that calls for a 50 percent reduction in CFC production by the end of 1998.

Part of the AT&T effort includes research into CFC alternatives such as BIOACT EC-7, a biodegradable solvent derived from oranges and wood pulp. As a result of its efforts on CFC reduction, AT&T was awarded the Council on Economic Priorities's Corporate Conscience Award in March of 1990.

Adopting External Measures and Protocols

A key aspect of exceeding environmental compliance levels is a willingness to adopt exacting standards for environmental performance established by an industry or third-party organization. For example, corporate membership in the Chemical Manufacturers Association includes the obligation to abide by the goals of that organization's "Responsible Care" program, which sets forth guiding health and environment principles and management practices for chemical manufacturers (see Table 1.1 and also Chapter 7).

Another industry-supported organization, Global Environmental Management Initiative (GEMI), promotes leadership in environmental management from within the business community. The organization was founded in 1990 by a work group of the Business Roundtable, which includes 200 chief executives representing a broad spectrum of industries. More than 240 companies, government agencies, and organizations attended GEMI's first conference (January 1991), which applied the concept of total quality management to corporate environmental strategies.

GEMI continues to foster ways in which businesses can work to develop environmental solutions through publications, annual conferences, and workgroups. The workgroups, listed below, are fundamental to GEMI's goal of providing specific tools, information, and solutions that address environmental problems in the business community.

- **Total Quality Environmental Management Workgroup.** Purpose: to stimulate, assemble, and promote worldwide critical thinking on environmental management.

21

TABLE 1.1
RESPONSIBLE CARE PROGRAM GUIDING PRINCIPLES

1. To recognize and respond to community concerns about chemicals and our operations.

2. To develop and produce chemicals that can be manufactured, transported, used and disposed of safely.

3. To make health, safety, and environmental considerations a priority in our planning for all existing and new products and processes.

4. To report promptly to officials, employees, customers and the public, information on chemical-related health or environmental hazards and to recommend protective measures.

5. To counsel customers on the safe use, transportation and disposal of chemical products.

6. To operate our plants and facilities in a manner that protects the environment and the health and safety of our employees and the public.

7. To extend knowledge by conducting or supporting research on the health, safety and environmental effects of our products, processes and waste materials.

8. To work with others to resolve problems created by past handling and disposal of hazardous substances.

9. To participate with government and others in creating responsible laws, regulations and standards to safeguard the community, workplace and environment.

10. To promote the principles and practices of Responsible Care by sharing experiences and offering assistance to others who produce, handle, use, transport or dispose of chemicals.

- **International Workgroup.** Purpose: to promote and develop tools and partnerships that help all industry segments implement the International Chamber of Commerce (ICC) principles of environmental management.

- **Stakeholder Communications Workgroup.** Purpose: to improve the content of environmental communications with interested parties.

- **Domestic Partnerships/Outreach Workgroup.** Purpose: to build GEMI's credibility and influence through visibility of results.

- **Data Measurement Workgroup.** Purpose: to stimulate, assemble, and promote worldwide critical self-assessment of corporate environmental management.

In addition to following the principles of organizations such as CMA and GEMI, corporations can agree to adhere to the "CERES Principles," developed by the Coalition for Environmentally Responsible Economics (CERES). The CERES Principles (see Table 1.2) are designed to help investors make decisions based on environmental considerations. They also serve as a "voluntary mechanism of corporate self-governance." CERES received a major boost in 1993 when Sun Company, Inc. agreed to adopt the principles.

According to David Sand, the project director for the CERES Principles and an analyst at Commonwealth Capital Partners of Cambridge, Massachusetts, which consults to CERES: "The guidelines for corporate environmental principles can be thought of as three concentric circles. The inner circle contains the company's own initiatives regarding environmental performance. The second circle contains industry-specific standards, such as the Chemical Manufacturers Association's Responsible Care program. The outer circle is a set of codes that crosses all companies and industries, the CERES Principles."

23

TABLE 1.2
THE CERES PRINCIPLES (Formerly the Valdez Principles)

Introduction

By adopting these Principles, we publicly affirm our belief that corporations have a responsibility for the environment, and must conduct all aspects of their business as responsible stewards of the environment by operating in a manner that protects the Earth. We believe that corporations must not compromise the ability of future generations to sustain themselves.

We will update our practices constantly in light of advances in technology and new understandings in health and environmental science. In collaborations with CERES, we will promote a dynamic process to ensure that the Principles are interpreted in a way that accommodates changing technologies and environmental realities. We intend to make consistent, measurable progress in implementing these Principles and to apply them to all aspects of our operations throughout the world.

Protection of the Biosphere

We will reduce and make continual progress toward eliminating the release of any substance that may cause environmental damage to the air, water, or the earth or its inhabitants. We will safeguard all habitats affected by our operations and will protect open spaces and wilderness, while preserving biodiversity.

Sustainable Use of Natural Resources

We will make sustainable use of renewable natural resources, such as water, soils and forests. We will conserve nonrenewable natural resources through efficient use and careful planning.

Reduction and Disposal of Waste

We will reduce and where possible eliminate waste through source reduction and recycling. All waste will be handled and disposed of through safe and responsible methods.

Energy Conservation

We will conserve energy and improve the energy efficiency of our internal operations and of the goods and services we sell. We will make every effort to use environmentally safe and sustainable energy sources.

TABLE 1.2   Continued

Risk Reduction
We will strive to minimize the environmental, health and safety risks to our employees and the communities in which we operate through safe technologies, facilities and operating procedures, and by being prepared for emergencies.

Safe Products and Services
We will reduce and where possible eliminate the use, manufacture or sale of products and services that cause environmental damage or health or safety hazards. We will inform our customers of the environmental impacts of our products or services and try to correct unsafe use.

Environmental Restoration
We will promptly and responsibly correct conditions we have caused that endanger health, safety or the environment. To the extent feasible, we will redress injuries we have caused to persons or damage we have caused to the environment and will restore the environment.

Informing the Public
We will inform in a timely manner everyone who may be affected by conditions caused by our company that might endanger health, safety or the environment. We will regularly seek advice and counsel through dialogue with persons in communities near our facilities. We will not take any action against employees for reporting dangerous incidents or conditions to management or to appropriate authorities.

Management Commitment
We will implement these Principles and sustain a process that ensures that the Board of Directors and Chief Executive Officer are fully informed about pertinent environmental issues and are fully responsible for environmental policy. In selecting our Board of Directors, we will consider demonstrated environmental commitment as a factor.

Audits and Reports
We will conduct an annual self-evaluation of our progress in implementing these Principles. We will support the timely creation of generally accepted environmental audit procedures. We will annually complete the CERES Report, which will be made available to the public.

25

TABLE 1.2   Continued

Disclaimer

These principles establish an environmental ethic with criteria by which investors and others can assess the environmental performance of companies. Companies that sign these Principles pledge to go voluntarily beyond the requirements of the law. These Principles are not intended to create new legal liabilities, expand existing rights or obligations, waive legal defenses, or otherwise affect the legal position of any signatory company, and are not intended to be used against a signatory in any legal proceeding for any purpose.

This amended version of the CERES Principles was adopted by the CERES Board of Directors on April 28, 1992.

Companies that wish to support the CERES Principles submit a written commitment to comply with the guidelines, one of which ("Audits and Reports") is a further commitment to conduct and make public an annual self-evaluation of the company's progress in implementing the principles and in complying with applicable laws and regulations throughout its worldwide application.

The method for performing the self-evaluation is to complete the exhaustive CERES audit form. The CERES audit is the environmental analog of the corporate financial disclosure—the "other bottom line." The coalition intends to print an annual report based on the environmental performance reports of its signatories. Perhaps in the future, vanguard environmentalist companies will produce 'double bottom line' annual reports as a standard business practice.

WORK WITH THE SURROUNDING COMMUNITY TO SOLVE ENVIRONMENTAL PROBLEMS

Companies with the best environmental track records tend to work closely with the surrounding community and organizations dedicated to bringing about positive environmental change. The most well-publicized of these alliances has been the one between McDonald's, which once ranked high on the hit list of conservationist organizations because of its wasteful packaging, and the Environmental Defense Fund, an activist organization that has brought numerous successful suits against private companies and the federal government (see Chapter 7).

But throughout the country, other companies are also working with local community groups and governments on issues such as household hazardous waste. In fact, a growing trend is to underwrite household hazardous waste collections in what are known as "Amnesty Days," which enable companies to help individuals dispose of toxic materials such as pesticides, paints, used motor oil, and other substances that should not be disposed of in town landfills (see Chapter 6 for details). More than just a "super trash collection," Amnesty Day events provide an opportunity for corporations to teach residents about the proper handling and use of household products containing dangerous substances. And their cost is minimal when compared to the goodwill benefits that the company accrues.

The opportunities to work with stakeholders are enormous and can be tailored to the unique interests and capabilities of any company. Pacific Gas & Electric, for example, is bringing its expertise in energy conservation directly to the public at its new Pacific Energy Center. This 25,000-square-foot facility provides information and education to professionals and the general public on the latest conservation technologies. According to project manager Kathleen Cruise, the Center is unique because "it will show how all [conservation] technologies integrate with each other."

In another project, PG&E combined social and environmental goals when it launched a youth program in which inner-city teenagers help plant trees around office buildings. PG&E donated the trees and worked closely with city officials

27

to administer the program, demonstrating that utility companies can give back to the community, too.

Gillette has demonstrated how companies can take a leading role in providing communities with "castoffs" (packing and other materials that would normally be slated for disposal). For example, one Boston site has donated pallets of unused caps from shaving cream canisters. Another Gillette site contributed two truckloads of packing materials. The castoffs are sent to the "Recycle Center," a project of The Institute for Self-Active Education. Teachers, students, and parents can visit the Center and collect all sorts of unusual (and safe) items that can be used in creative play. Gillette is not only a contributor to the Center but also formed an advisory committee of retired executives who viewed the Institute's plans to open Recycle Centers in other cities. (At the time of this writing, 11 centers were in operation.)

According to Walter Drew, director of the Institute: "The Recycle Center is a unique cost-effective process for utilizing ecologically what would otherwise be solid waste to develop our most precious resources—our children. Corporations are often not aware of the significant contribution their cast-off materials can make. If anything, they express initial surprise that they have anything to contribute. But what treasures they're sitting on!"

Programs such as Gillette's are more than nice gestures—they communicate a strong message to all stakeholders that the company is not just in business to make a profit. Rather, they create win-win situations for the company (reduced disposal bills), the community (free materials for its schools), and the environment (reduced burden on landfill space).

Finally, as you'll see in the next chapter, total quality environmental management ultimately strives for better relationships with your internal and external customers. With environmental issues, everyone who breathes your air or does business with you is a customer. Treat them right, and your company has its best chances of gaining a competitive edge and prospering under any economic conditions.

BUILDING A FOUNDATION FOR ENVIRONMENTAL ACTION

1. The strongest incentives to create an environmentally sound company flow from the top down; make sure the message from the top is as strong as possible.

2. People are the most valuable asset in any company's effort to solve environmental problems and prevent new ones in the future.

3. Every strategic decision has an environmental impact; make sure that the environment is factored into your strategic planning process.

4. Adopt standards far beyond those associated with compliance; you'll stand out as an environmental leader in your industry.

5. The surrounding community and other stakeholders outside your corporation are your environmental "customers"—give them top-notch service, and you'll reap the rewards of a satisfied customer base.

CHAPTER 2

TOTAL QUALITY ENVIRONMENTAL MANAGEMENT

Using TQEM to Create an Environmentally Sound Organization

Form, fit, and function—these concepts have traditionally defined the well-designed product. Today, "well-designed" also connotes measures of environmental quality such as disassembly, remanufacture, reuse, recycling, and final disposition. Moreover, companies today must strive for measurable, demonstrable environmental improvement, the kind that results from using total quality environmental management (TQEM).

TQEM is a specific application of the proven principles of total quality management (TQM)—an effort spearheaded by the Global Environmental Management Initiative (GEMI) to provide a systematic approach and methodology for continuous improvement in environmental performance.

This chapter begins with a brief explanation of the principles of TQM and then explains the special applications of the management approach to environmental issues. Whereas Chapter 1 introduced the foundations for corporate environmental programs, this chapter introduces the important management perspectives needed to implement those programs. The themes inherent in total quality management and continuous improvement provide the basis for the implementation of programs and practices to be introduced throughout this book.

TQM BASICS

According to *Quality Progress*, a publication of the American Society for Quality Control, total quality management "is a management approach to long-term success through customer satisfaction. TQM is based on the participation of all members of an organization in improving processes, products, services, and the culture they work in."

The definition reveals several key elements of TQM (and hence TQEM):

■ It is a *management* approach.

■ It is a *long-term* process.

■ It *involves everyone* in the organization.

■ It is based on *continuous improvement*.

The definition also reflects an accumulation of knowledge about quality improvement whose origins can be traced to the period just after World War II. At that time, the shortage of consumer goods focused every manufacturer's attention on producing volume. American managers, determined to produce as much as possible and as quickly as they could, relegated quality control to an end-of-the-line, inspect-and-test function. Quality suffered as the drive to increase quantities grew.

Japan had a different problem. Before the war, Japan's military leaders channeled significant resources into developing a powerful military machine. Its civilian economy had a lower priority that led to cheap and shoddy products. In the postwar era, the leaders of Japan's major companies recognized that their survival depended on their civilian goods and exports. That created an imperative to rebuild factories while creating a revolution in quality. Japanese leaders looked for help from the experts who had worked on improving the quality of U.S. military products, one of whom was Homer Sarasohn, a systems and electronics engineer. During a 250-hour course, Sarasohn taught Japan's senior executives and managers the fundamentals of quality systems thinking. Other American experts in this field, most notably W. Edwards Deming and J.M. Juran, worked with Japanese managers to develop and refine a system for continuous quality improvement.

Based on what they learned, the Japanese identified decisive strategies for creating a revolution in quality. Juran describes four of them in his pathbreaking book, *Juran on Leadership for Quality*:

1. The upper managers personally took charge of leading the revolution.

2. All levels and functions underwent training in managing for quality.

3. Quality improvement was undertaken at a continuous, revolutionary pace.

4. The work force was enlisted in quality improvement through the QC-circle concept.

These strategies correspond with the definition of total quality management presented earlier in this chapter: a process that is led by management, involves everyone, and is based on continuous improvement. By using this process, the Japanese have been able to systematically improve the excellence of their products and manufacturing techniques during the past 40 years. Although many American companies have been motivated by the Japanese to improve quality, the greatest inspiration for a national quality revolution in the United States has been the Malcolm Baldrige National Quality Award.

Created by the Malcolm Baldrige National Quality Improvement Act of 1987, this award program is aimed at increasing the quality and productivity of U.S. companies. The act called for "establishing guidelines and criteria that can be used by business, industrial, governmental, and other organizations in evaluating their own quality improvement efforts." The criteria, developed by and refined with input from the nation's leading quality professionals, have become a national model for TQM in the United States.

Companies that use the criteria to implement the TQM approach enjoy a variety of benefits, including better relationships with their customers and better internal communication and teamwork. People who work in companies where there is a strong TQM presence feel empowered and inspired. All efforts are channeled into a single, unifying goal: continuous quality improvement.

TQEM BASICS

TQEM, like TQM, requires a systems approach. No company can move toward environmental excellence with a hit-or-miss, reactionary strategy. As George Carpenter, GEMI chairman and director of environment, energy, and safety systems at

Procter & Gamble, commented at GEMI's first conference: "Total quality begins with accepting that we are never as good as we can be. Continuous improvement based on data and measurement is the fundamental bedrock of total quality. Thus, with total quality we have an explainable, understandable, and documentable path to implement pollution prevention and improve every aspect of our environmental management."

"Pollution is a defect," says Tom Zosel, 3M's manager of pollution prevention programs. "Our goal is zero defects, in the same way that the goal in our quality process is zero defects. Pollution prevention fits very well because the concepts are exactly the same."

The focus of TQEM is on shifting environmental goals from compliance to customer satisfaction. In these times of growing environmental awareness, customers expect businesses to protect their health and preserve the environment. "Once you understand how total quality applies to the environment, it's no different than total quality applied to every other aspect of a business," says Carpenter. "GEMI is helping people make the paradigm shift."

To understand how TQEM functions, we need to return to the definition of TQM stated earlier: "a management approach to long-term success through customer satisfaction. . . . based on the participation of all members of an organization in improving processes, products, services, and the culture they work in." By looking at each essential ingredient in TQM, we can see how TQEM is deployed at companies like Xerox, 3M, Procter & Gamble, Merck, Eastman Kodak, and DuPont.

TQEM: Led by Management

TQM and TQEM are management-led processes. According to the Baldrige criteria: "A company's senior leaders must create clear and visible quality values and high expectations. Reinforcement of the values and expectations requires their substantial personal commitment and involvement." Leaders in environmental management are guided by clear, visible statements of environmental values, usually in the form of mission statements prominently displayed throughout their facilities.

Creating Environmental Policies

Xerox won the Baldrige Award in 1989. It has incorporated environmental management into its TQM process through a precise environmental policy:

> Xerox Corporation is committed to the protection of the environment and the health and safety of its employees, customers and neighbors. This commitment is applied worldwide in developing new products and processes.

The policy embraces four basic principles:

1. Environmental health and safety concerns take priority over economic considerations.

2. All Xerox operations must conduct themselves in a manner that safeguards health, protects the environment, and conserves valuable materials and resources.

3. Xerox is committed to the continual improvement of its performance in environmental protection and resource conservation, both in company operations and in the design of its products.

4. Xerox is committed to designing its products for optimal recyclability and reuse. Xerox is equally committed to taking every opportunity to recycle or reuse waste materials generated by its operations.

3M's board of directors adopted the following corporate environmental policy on February 10, 1975:

3M will continue to recognize and exercise its responsibility to:

- Solve its own environmental pollution and conservation problems.

- Prevent pollution at the source.

- Develop products that will have a minimum effect on the environment.

- Conserve natural resources through the use of reclamation and other appropriate methods.

- Assure that its facilities and products meet and sustain the regulations of all federal, state and local environmental agencies.

- Assist, wherever possible, governmental agencies and other official organizations engaged in environmental activities.

The policy provided direction for the company's environmental management process, most notably its "Pollution Prevention Pays" program.

McDonald's follows an environmental policy created by a joint task force consisting of members from McDonald's and the Environmental Defense Fund (see Chapter 7). The policy states that "McDonald's believes it has a special responsibility to protect our environment for future generations. . . . We will lead, both in word and in deed." The policy further states that the company is guided by four principles: effectively managing solid waste, conserving and protecting natural resources, encouraging environmental values and practices, and ensuring accountability procedures.

Procter & Gamble's Environmental Quality Policy is more specific:

Procter & Gamble is committed to providing products of superior quality and value that best fill the needs of the world's consumers. As part of this, Procter & Gamble continually strives to improve the environmental quality of its products, packaging, and operations around the world. To carry out this commitment, it is Procter & Gamble's policy to:

■ Ensure our products, packaging, and operations are safe for our employees, consumers and the environment.

■ Reduce or prevent the environmental impact of our products and packaging in their design, manufacture, distribution, use and disposal whenever possible.

■ Meet or exceed the requirements of all environmental laws and regulations.

■ Continually assess our environmental technology and programs, and monitor progress toward environmental goals.

■ Provide our consumers, customers, employees, communities, public interest groups and others with relevant and appropriate factual information about the environmental quality of Procter & Gamble products, packaging, and operations.

■ Ensure every employee understands and is responsible and accountable for incorporating environmental considerations in daily business activities.

■ Have operating policies, programs and resources in place to implement our environmental quality policy.

The policy, presented in a brochure that outlines Procter & Gamble's TQEM approach, is followed by a statement by the company's chairman and chief executive officer affirming the importance of the company's role in developing solutions to environmental problems.

Conducting Environmental Training

The affirmation of the importance of environmental goals is a critical second step in this management-led process. Having a clear and visible environmental policy is not enough; it must be constantly reinforced by senior management's personal commitment and involvement.

Such a commitment often includes training in environmental management and participation on a corporate environmental quality committee. The training familiarizes managers with environmental issues and how they relate to their company, suggests a process for managing those issues, and explains the tools needed to work the process. For companies involved in total quality management, this often means relating TQM training to environmental management. Managers who have learned how to use statistical and problem solving tools to improve quality find it easy to apply those skills to environmental issues.

Forming Environmental Steering Committees

The purpose of creating a senior-level environmental steering committee is to help all employees recognize that environmental management is a corporate issue affecting everyone. The committee can have a variety of responsibilities, including:

- Providing direction for the company's environmental management process.

- Establishing measures that the company can use to determine performance.

- Monitoring progress on achieving environmental goals and adjusting the policy, goals, or course to keep the company on target.

- Communicating goals as well as processes to achieve them and progress toward them to all employees.

- Chairing cross-functional teams focused on company-wide environmental issues.

At the Eastman Kodak Company, the management committee on environmental responsibility is chaired by the CEO. Its chief responsibility is to articulate Kodak's environmental policies, principles, and performance standards worldwide (see Chapter 3 for details).

Xerox formed a senior management Environmental Leadership Steering Committee in late 1990. The committee, which includes senior representatives from major functional groups and worldwide operating companies, meets quarterly to focus on and resolve environmental program content and funding issues.

Procter & Gamble's Environmental Quality Team reflects the company's evolution from delegating environmental issues to support groups to integrating them into corporate planning and decision making. The multisector team, which includes representatives from all major functional areas, meets every two weeks for about three hours to make sure all functions are moving in the same direction and to develop strategies, policies, and guidelines. Their recommendations are submitted to senior management for consideration as company policy.

3M elevated its environmental decisions to the senior boardroom by changing its corporate structure, putting environmental engineering on the same level with its other operating units. According to L.D. Simone, chairman and chief executive officer: "The next effect is that environmental concerns are considered at every step in the development and manufacture of our products. This assures upper management that our goals of environmental protection are being met." 3M's senior managers are required to incorporate the company's environmental policies, objectives, and standards into their operations. Summary progress reports are presented each month to the corporate operations committee. Each operating division has an environmental management plan that guides division operations for the short- and long-term, providing for the efficient allocation of resources.

TQEM: Long-Term Process

TQM and TQEM are long-term processes. The goal is continuous improvement toward the ideal of zero defects or zero pollution. 3M has been working its Pollution Prevention Pays program since 1975. Gillette formalized its process to conserve energy and water in 1972. They and others are quick to point out that environmental management, like total quality management, requires long-term thinking.

In 1990 Merck & Company, a manufacturer of health products and specialty chemicals, developed a five-year strategic plan that guides the company's environmental activities worldwide. A cross-functional team of corporate executives built the plan around three corporate goals aimed at dramatically reducing releases of toxic chemicals by the end of 1995.

Merck used its strategic planning process to define environmental policy and ensure its acceptance and implementation throughout the company. At the conclusion of the process, the planning team compiled a list of lessons learned for companies about to embark on similar processes:

41

1. Get attention at the top. Once again, the process is led by management.

2. Work overtime but set a time limit. Merck completed its plan in six months, which required the team to hold day-long work sessions at least once a week for several months and to participate in subcommittee meetings, in addition to its regular work.

3. Limit the number of core planners. Fewer people makes it easier to create a clear, concise plan.

4. Promote dialogue between business and environmental health and safety professionals. The exchange of perspectives and ideas builds trust and understanding.

5. Include planning professionals. Planning experts acting as facilitator and resources can help keep the process moving and on track.

TQEM: Customer Satisfaction

The ultimate goal of the environmental planning process is customer satisfaction. Most quality leaders define *customers* as the people who actually purchase their products and services, as well as their shareholders, employees, suppliers, and surrounding communities. In the case of environmental issues, customers must also include local, state, and federal regulatory bodies.

Procter & Gamble credits its success to its ability to listen to consumers and recognize and meet their needs. Consumers have been telling Procter & Gamble that they want products that are compatible with their environmental concerns. That makes environmental issues a business need and an opportunity for competitive advantage. "If we meet this new need first and best, in an ethically sound way, consumers will buy our products in preference over our competitors','' said Deborah Anderson, Procter & Gamble's Vice President of Environmental Quality, at a conference on the environment sponsored by *BusinessWeek* and the World Resources Institute.

The company's environmental achievements confirm its commitment to meeting consumers' environmental needs. All of Procter & Gamble's plastic bottles are now coded for recycling. All Spic and Span Pine bottles are made entirely of recycled soft-drink bottles. Its concentrated laundry detergents reduce packaging; Downy refills, for example, use 75 percent less packaging material than the plastic Downy bottle. New packaging technology has eliminated the outside cartons for Procter & Gamble's deodorants, saving 3.4 million pounds of solid waste each year. And, in response to ongoing concerns over disposable diapers and solid waste in general, Procter & Gamble has committed $20 million to support pilot solid waste composting programs nationwide.

Procter & Gamble's efforts exemplify a core Baldrige value: ''Customer-driven quality . . . demands constant sensitivity to emerging customer and market requirements.'' The first steps in Xerox's quality improvement process are identifying the output, the customer, and the customers' requirements. In this way, the company's primary objective of customer satisfaction is established early in the process. As employees work on an environmental quality issue, all efforts are ultimately channeled back to the goal of customer satisfaction.

TQEM: Employee Involvement

Employee involvement is the key to successful, long-term environmental management. In a speech to the Edison Electric Institute Energy and Environment Committee in late 1991,

Alison Silverstein, a senior analyst for Pacific Gas & Electric, remarked: "Ninety percent of PG&E's employees call themselves environmentalists. All of those employees are PG&E shareholders. This tells us that it is not going to take much for our employees to internalize the environmental goals and operating assumptions that we value. It is the energy and continuing involvement and creativity of those employees that will ensure the success of PG&E's environmental policy."

Employee involvement makes environmental management possible. One of TQM's cornerstones is that full participation by all employees is necessary for continuous improvement. Quality is not restricted to certain processes, products, services, divisions, groups, or individuals; it is an element of every task performed by every employee.

Edward Woolard, chairman and chief executive officer of E.I. du Pont de Nemours, Inc., made this comment in *Managing the Global Environmental Challenge*, a report published by Business International Corporation: "As long as environmental protection remains in a special category assigned to certain people—instead of part of the mental checklist with which each person approaches every task—then our environmental accomplishments will remain reactive and corrective rather than proactive and innovative."

Xerox involves all of its employees in its "Leadership through Quality" process, of which environmental quality improvement is a part. The company has trained all of its employees in the use of statistical, problem solving, and teamwork tools, and it encourages employees to form Quality Improvement Teams to address quality—and environmental—issues.

"Any employee at Xerox has the power to form a team," says Abhay Bhushan, Xerox's manager of environmental leadership programs. "I see employees as agents of change. Most people want to do something good. If they can help the environment and save the company money, it's human nature to feel happier." Xerox has noticed that employee enthusiasm for projects that include environmental benefits is generally higher than that for other types of projects.

Employees who have been empowered by TQM welcome the opportunity to participate in environmental protection. "We put our Pollution Prevention Pays program to our people as an opportunity to bring their environmental activism into their day-to-day jobs," says Tom Zosel, 3M's manager of pollution prevention programs. "That's the best way to keep things going."

TQEM: Continuous Improvement

The final element in the definition of a TQM approach involves extending the improvement process into the future. According to the Baldrige criteria: "Achieving the highest levels of quality and competitiveness requires a well-defined and well-executed approach to continuous improvement, a process which must contain regular cycles of planning, execution, and evaluation."

Procter & Gamble's approach is to use the continuous improvement cycle—Plan, Do, Check, Act (PDCA)—to improve its environmental systems and programs.

Plan: P&G uses assessments, goal setting, and benchmarking to plan pollution out of its processes, products, and packaging.

Do: P&G relies on process control and pollution prevention programs to reduce scrap, rework, energy, and discharges to the environment.

Check: P&G uses quality tools and environmental audits to analyze data, quantify results, and understand successes and failures.

Act: P&G establishes standards and conducts training to institute systems that will sustain the improvements and to deploy the systems between sites, brands, and divisions.

The process is then repeated in the ongoing pursuit of zero defects. "PDCA is fundamental to total quality management," says Procter & Gamble's George Carpenter. "It's a way of thinking and looking at a problem that can be used by individuals and teams in every department."

OBSTACLES TO TQEM

Few companies are prepared for the concept of senior executives leading a long-term approach to achieving customer satisfaction through the involvement of all employees in continuous environmental quality improvement. Fewer still feel able to commit to the depth of cultural change and technical advancement that this concept requires. Therefore, before adopting a TQEM program, be aware of the following obstacles:

- **Lack of a perceived reason to pursue TQEM.** The adoption of TQEM represents an enormous change, one that can only be realized when a company feels compelled to make it. If the urgency and commitment are missing, the tendency will be to work on issues currently on the table by using procedures and tools that have worked in the past.

- **Top management's lack of involvement.** The greatest obstacle is a lack of understanding and participation by top management. If senior managers are not personally

46

involved in learning about environmental issues, providing broad direction for the company's environmental activities and participating in councils, committees, or teams devoted to environmental management, there is little chance of success.

- **A short-term focus.** There is always the temptation to reduce a major change to banners and slogans that blur the need for steady improvement. Long-term success is not possible with a "program of the month" approach; it requires deep-rooted change.

- **Less-than-total employee involvement.** TQEM flounders when the responsibility for it is limited to an environmental department or manager. As quality leaders have shown, quality improvement is everyone's job. Environmental quality improvement must be every employee's responsibility.

- **The absence of reliable data and information.** TQEM begins with an assessment of a company's current environmental management program and proceeds with the analysis of data and information that accurately depicts the company's environmental performance. The absence of this data and information makes it impossible to evaluate progress or make wise business decisions.

- **A limiting definition of** *customers*. Until recently, the environmentalist "customers" that needed to be satisfied were government regulatory agencies. A TQEM program that focuses only on them will fail, because today's environmentalist customers include employees, suppliers, community members, conservationist groups, and the people who buy your products and services. Your company must be clear about the needs and expectations of

47

all of its environmentally conscious customers for TQEM to work.

All of these obstacles should be addressed by a well-conceived plan that leads to employee training, empowerment, and involvement. TQEM demands management by fact. And it is consistent in its focus on knowing and satisfying all customers. Companies that are taking the lead in environmental quality management consider the above obstacles as opportunities to sharpen their focus on customers, to involve senior management in a critical issue, to plan for long-term success, and to increase employee involvement.

BENEFITS OF TQEM

The benefits of implementing TQEM mirror the benefits of implementing TQM:

- **Improved customer satisfaction.** Whether your customers are regulatory agencies, consumers, community members, or employees, a systematic approach to managing environmental quality will improve your relationships with them.

- **Improved organizational effectiveness.** TQEM demands the involvement of all employees in improving environmental quality. For employees to be effective, they must be trained. Communication and teamwork must improve. All efforts must focus on a single goal visibly supported by senior management. As a result, the entire company moves as one on a shared mission.

- **Improved competitiveness.** The companies discussed in this chapter are using TQEM to improve their competitive position. Procter & Gamble's director of environmental coordination points out that if P&G's products are compatible with consumers' environmental concerns, "consumers will buy our products in preference over our competitors." Also, the ability of companies cited in this book to significantly cut costs by reducing the need for environmental remediation lowers their manufacturing costs, making their products more competitive.

How To Implement TQEM

Companies that are enjoying the benefits of TQEM identify four key steps that must be taken to implement a successful program:

1. Assess your environmental status.

2. Establish an environmental mission, policy, and short- and long-range objectives.

3. Train employees in the quality improvement process and the use of quality tools.

4. Identify the needs and expectations of your external and internal customers.

Let's consider each step of the implementation process.

Assessments

No company can improve without a clear understanding of its existing environmental management system. Companies gain this understanding by evaluating performance and practice at all facilities.

Assessments constitute one of the key activities in Kodak's environmental management program. The company conducts two assessment types: 1) compliance assessments, which are used to monitor operations in the context of corporate policies, principles, and standards as well as compliance with laws and regulations; and 2) risk assessments, which are conducted to anticipate potential problems and hazards. Where gaps exist between expectations and performance, Kodak helps its line managers design programs to close them.

Xerox conducts environmental audits annually, although the frequency varies with the nature of the facility; manufacturing plants are audited more often than administrative offices. "Facilities know they can be audited at any time," says Bhushan, "but the facility is notified before all regular audits. This is better because the idea is improvement, not finding fault or blaming. If they correct something because they know they're getting audited, that's good, because prevention is always better than the cure."

Procter & Gamble audits all of its 150 facilities worldwide annually. "We have a system that scores a set of key elements on a 10-point scale and the scores are tracked on a corporate basis," says Carpenter. "It's a system audit, not a compliance audit. We use it to identify where we need to focus our attention, within a plant, in a certain business sector, or in a part of the world."

A typical audit begins with notifying the site, choosing the audit team, and planning the visit. At the site, the audit team interviews key people and reviews documents and data to understand the environmental management system. The team identifies strengths and weaknesses and gathers evidence. The audit team then compiles its findings in a report that is usually outlined verbally to the facility's management and then written in more detail in an audit report. Plant management responds to the report by developing an action plan that addresses the weaknesses that were discovered. "An action plan comes out of each of our audits," says Procter & Gamble's Carpenter. "The audit team, which includes plant members, prepares the action plan. Progress is reviewed a couple months later.''

Policy

The United States' best TQEM role models have built their systems upon clearly stated, widely accepted environmental policies and objectives. Several examples were provided earlier in this chapter. Xerox, Procter & Gamble, McDonald's, 3M, and others communicate their environmental policies frequently and consistently through internal newsletters and correspondence and through the actions of their senior executives and managers.

Training

Quality leaders invest in quality training. Motorola, which won the Baldrige Award in 1988, has an annual education budget of $60 million. IBM Rochester, a Baldrige Award winner in 1990, spends an amount equal to 5 percent of its payroll on training. Milliken, a 1989 Baldrige Award winner, averages 76 hours of quality training per employee per year. These and other quality leaders recognize the need to prepare people for the challenge of continuous improvement.

By contrast, many companies thrust employees into the environmental arena without giving them the tools they need to be effective. A commitment to environmental quality is not enough; employees must be prepared through training to work in teams, solve problems, and initiate improvements.

Quality training focuses on statistical theory and tools, problem-solving skills, and team skills, all of which are effective for any type of issue that a company may address, including environmental ones. Companies typically start by teaching the basics of the quality improvement process and then introducing tools, such as Pareto and control charts and benchmarking, that employees can put to immediate use.

Customers

As with all quality improvement activities, the focus of environmental quality improvement is on achieving customer satisfaction. Every company, division, department, and individual must understand that environmental quality is judged by the customer. As Procter & Gamble, 3M, Xerox, and others have shown, the most compelling reason to implement TQEM is customer satisfaction. To initiate your program, use every tool available to collect information about your customers' needs and expectations and then organize that information according to your company's most pressing priorities.

5 STEPS TO BECOMING A TQEM LEADER

1. Learn all you can about TQM and TQEM. Benchmarking other companies is an excellent way to find out what quality leaders are doing in the environmental arena. The companies discussed in this chapter and book provide a good starting point.

2. Make TQEM a corporate mission. Write about it. Talk about it. Promote it. Reward people for it. Teach it. Participate in it. And do anything else you can to show your commitment to the process.

3. Help every employee feel responsible for TQEM. Environmental quality improvement takes place incrementally as employees learn quality improvement skills and apply those skills to their jobs. Total quality improvement is only possible when everyone participates in the process.

4. Know what your environmentally conscious customers want and make sure you give it to them.

5. Pursue TQEM relentlessly! Interest will flag. Goals will blur. Distractions will appear. The pursuit of TQEM will slow, but you must keep it on track. When others lose sight of your environmental mission, wave it proudly and call them to action. When they tire, praise their achievements and remind them of their progress. As quality leaders have shown, the pursuit of total quality produces a wealth of success stories about individuals, teams, departments, divisions, and the company. Use these real benefits to inspire your company's never-ending pursuit of total quality environmental management.

CHAPTER 3

UP THE ENVIRONMENTAL ORGANIZATION
Building a "Green" Culture

On October 16, 1989, each employee of the Boston-head-quartered Fidelity Brokerage Services received a memo from CEO Edward C. Johnson III that outlined the company's new environmental program. Most Fidelity people found it novel enough to receive a memo from Johnson, who was not a particularly public figure; those who had E-mail were shocked when they arrived at work a week later and found a message from Johnson, urging them to make the program work. This unusual use of E-mail for a company-wide communication at Fidelity apparently had an impact; the program handsomely exceeded its recycling goals for the year.

As in the case of Fidelity, an environmental "call to arms" from the CEO can mobilize a company into action. But although the CEO can send a clear signal to everyone in the company, someone must have the clout to translate top management's policies into specific programs, monitor progress through audits, and enforce compliance. In manufacturing companies, this is generally the domain of an environmental officer who serves on the senior management team. In service and nonmanufacturing companies, the job of turning environmental policy into action often lands on the property or building manager's desk, although an increasing number of service companies are creating special environmental officer positions.

In addition to having top-level support and a means for establishing working environmental programs, to succeed with environmental issues a company must have the means of harnessing its employees' environmental know-how gained from practical experience at home, the media, and popular books. This often means sanctioning employee "Green Teams" that identify environmental problems and opportunities and then work with management to put appropriate programs in place.

This chapter covers models for senior managers charged with managing environmental issues and describes the "care and feeding" of Green Teams. You'll read about several tried and proven environmental structures at major companies as well as tips and techniques for mobilizing the energies of employees committed to making their companies more environmentally responsible.

TACKLING FRONTLINE ENVIRONMENTAL ISSUES

In traditional "smokestack" companies, the health, safety, and environment officer handled all environmental issues. But as environmental concerns have broadened, many companies—manufacturing and service alike—have developed new approaches to environmental management.

In some companies, once technical positions have become more senior. At Gillette, for example, Dr. Robert Giovacchini, the corporate vice-president responsible for product integrity, reports directly to the chairman and has worldwide authority to stop production on any line when a particular process or product may pose a pollution or human health risk.

At Procter & Gamble, Dr. Deborah Anderson, Vice President of Environmental Quality, reports directly to the chairman and oversees all environmental policies for the global corporation. Every two weeks Anderson meets with a multifunctional team that includes representatives from all areas of the company—people in packaging, consumer researchers, advertising managers, manufacturing representatives, and product development engineers, to name a few. The group identifies needs for guidelines and submits them to senior management for approval and incorporation into company environmental policy. If Anderson believes that a course correction needs to be made at any level or at any location in Procter & Gamble, she addresses it directly with the people involved.

In addition to finding themselves with more sweeping oversight and jurisdiction, corporate environmental officers today are more likely to take an active role in the environmental arena. As described in Chapter 2, Procter & Gamble has been a driving force behind the establishment and growth of GEMI. According to George Carpenter, director of environment, energy, and safety systems at Procter & Gamble and the chairman of GEMI, corporate environmental professionals "know how to cause positive environmental change, both within their own businesses and within world business as a whole. This knowledge of how business works and accomplishes things is key to their success."

Beyond increasing the scope of environmental officers, many companies have evolved innovative organizational structures and created entirely new positions to best deal with the environmental issues unique to their particular industry. In the following section, we'll examine three very different approaches in three different industries.

The first of these, used at Kodak, represents a unified hierarchical approach well suited to a major manufacturer with multiple sites and extensive product lines, each with a potentially high environmental impact. The second, used at Apple Computer, illustrates how a "green issues manager" can work side by side with a health, safety, and environmental officer and solve problems that are beyond the latter's traditional sphere of responsibility. The third approach, typified by Gurasich, Spence, Darilek, and Mclure (GSD&M), shows how paper-based companies can evolve positions of environmental responsibility on an ad hoc basis and then formalize them into the organizational structure.

Kodak

Given its status as the world's principal supplier of film and processing chemicals as well as a manufacturer of numerous specialty products that run the gamut from pharmaceuticals to plastic for beverage bottles, Kodak faces enormous environmental challenges. All of its products have a significant environmental impact in their production and disposal, and the company has had to develop a unified approach to environmental quality that can be applied at its facilities at home and abroad.

To translate its environmental vision into action, Kodak has deployed a network of interlocking teams and working groups that develop and implement operational policies at all levels of the corporation. At the center is the Management Committee on Environmental Responsibility (MCER), which is chaired by the CEO and provides worldwide direction and review of environmental policies. The Public Policy Committee (PPC), which consists of outside members of the board of directors, reviews the company's policies and procedures and make recommendations to MCER.

Another body, the Health, Safety, and Environment Coordinating Committee (HSECC), provides technical advice and recommendations to MCER and the Public Policy Committee. It also develops and administers specific programs initiated by MCER. Part of HSECC's responsibility is to develop and disseminate Kodak's guiding principles and performance standards by means of: 1) prudent practice, 2) assessment of its performance and practice around the globe, and 3) training and educating all of its employees about the technical requirements and expectations of environmental policies at Kodak.

Finally, the Health and Environmental Laboratories (HAEL), with a staff of more than 200 people, provides HSECC with the resources for testing and assessment. The laboratory staff are literally on the front line, conducting audits and examining new materials for environmental and safety concerns.

HAEL also serves as a technical resource to a variety of Kodak groups, including the Eastman Chemical Company Health, Safety, and Environment Council; the European Health, Safety, and Environment Coordinating Committee; the Customer Imaging Environmental Support Services group; and numerous Business Unit and Regional Environmental Coordinating Teams.

Complex as this model may seem, it enables Kodak to maintain a uniform grip on the regulatory demands faced by a multinational chemical corporation and to meet the challenge of being a consumer products company serving ever more environmentally conscious consumers.

Apple Computer

As a manufacturer, Apple has always had a group responsible for ensuring the environmental integrity and safety of its manufacturing processes. In keeping with new, conservation-minded goals, top management determined that the company needed to explore the nature and extent of environmental impact of Apple's products after leaving the factory and reaching end users. This led to the creation of a new position, the green issues manager.

The green issues manager serves as a second product manager for Apple's various computer and printer lines. But instead of dealing with technical specifications and marketing considerations, the green issues manager is responsible for analyzing the environmental impact of each product and its packaging. For example, Apple's current green issues manager, Omar Kalisha, played a role in changing Apple product boxes from bleached white cardboard to unbleached stock. This is not only cheaper but also helps the environment in terms of reducing dioxin contamination at paper mills. (Dioxins are a by-product of the chlorine bleaching process used to whiten most papers. One well-known form of dioxin is Agent Orange, the defoliant used during the Vietnam War.)

Although switching to unbleached boxes may seem like a small step, it is part of an important new mind-set at Apple, one that Kalisha believes has implications for all of manufacturing: " 'Cradle-to-grave' analysis will become more a part of every company's approach to designing and manufacturing its products. As part of this thinking, companies must think in terms of a 'leasing model'—one way or another, products come back to you after you sell them. In other words, manufacturers are going to have to understand that they have a responsibility for the final disposition of the product."

Part of Kalisha's role as green issues manager is to effect

60

cross-industry education. "Suppliers must be made aware of "end of life issues" and the demands that manufacturers will be placing on them to provide products that can be reused or disposed of in an environmentally responsible fashion." The educational demands extend to customers as well. In the case of the unbleached boxes for product packaging, for instance, there is an important issue of "image." To make it work, Kalisha had to first convince the marketing managers that customers could not only be educated about the advantages of brown boxes but that they would see the change in a positive light.

While Kalisha is now accepted among the product groups, there were some initial concerns about the potential overlap of responsibilities between his domain and that of the environmental health and safety manager. As he points out: "There has been a certain sensitivity about stepping on other people's toes. You have to recognize that professionals in environment, health, and safety would like to get more involved with the products, but they're buried in their regular jobs and generally don't have the time for new responsibilities. The net effect of having both a green issues manager and a regular environment, health, and safety group has been to increase the overall visibility of environmental issues and to expand the resources available to the entire company."

Another sensitivity consideration involved the building of cross-functional relationships. According to Kalisha, there has to be a "genetic fit" between the green issues manager and the rest of the company. Kalisha must interact with people throughout the company, in sales, purchasing, engineering, design, manufacturing, and customer relations—just as a traditional product manager would. Communication channels are critical so that people do not perceive him as a source of additional work and compliance requirements.

As with all new environmental initiatives, a key element

in Apple's success with green issues management has been its explicit support by top management. Apple also has the kind of corporate culture that encourages interaction in cross-functional work groups while minimizing competitive conflicts between different functions within the organization. The same attitudes that made the development of the Macintosh computer a possibility are helping the company to make environmental responsibility a reality in an industry with significant effects on the environment at both the manufacturing and consumer ends of the spectrum.

GSD&M

The organizational chart of service or information companies does not generally include a box for an environmental manager; instead, office managers may get involved in purchasing recycled paper products, and building managers will often help set up recycling programs. In other cases, an ad hoc committee establishes a recycling program or responds to some other specific need, such as laser toner cartridge reclamation. Even so, "unofficial environmental officials" are springing up in service companies throughout the country as top management realizes the benefits to be gained by sanctioning an individual to manage such concerns full-time.

This was exactly the case at GSD&M, one of the nation's larger advertising agencies. In 1989, one of GSD&M's largest accounts, Walmart, asked the firm to explore the marketing implications of environmental issues. It soon became apparent to the staff at GSD&M that it had numerous opportunities right under its own roof to make a more environmentally responsible workplace. Managers from various departments, with the blessings of top management, established an informal team to investigate and report on potential actions that the company could take to curb pollution and waste.

The group, headed by Glenda Goehrs, then in charge of internal communications, began by calling a meeting of all "concerned employees" to brainstorm environmental concerns. "I didn't expect much of a turnout," she confesses. "In this business we tend to get a little tired of all the meetings. So I was pleasantly shocked when 38 people turned up."

GSD&M's top management enthusiastically supported the committee and sanctioned an environmental audit by a local nonprofit organization. The audit helped the company plan a paper recycling program, among other actions.

As the company's program got underway, Goehrs found herself becoming increasingly involved with ecological issues. With the support of top management, her responsibilities relating to new business development and internal communications were dropped, and she now serves as the company's vice-president of environmental affairs. In addition to expanding recycling and other programs, she created (and edits) an environmental newsletter that GSD&M makes available to current and prospective clients. Within GSD&M, Goehrs has also become an important resource for account executives who need to understand the environmental issues that their clients are currently facing or will face in the future. As a natural extension of her work with these concerns, Goehrs has also represented GSD&M in speaking engagements at professional and civic groups.

Through the investment of Goehrs's time and other resources, GSD&M has made a clear statement about its stand on the environment to both its employees and its clients. And although the direct payback in terms of internal savings is relatively small, the intangible value of the company's expertise in the environmental arena is immeasurable. It will only assist the company as more clients recognize the importance of developing and publicizing similar programs.

Kodak, Apple, and GSD&M represent three different approaches to environmental management, each suited to the scope and needs of the respective organizations. Clearly, when dealing with an operation the size of Kodak, a centralized means of maintaining compliance and providing technical resources is critical. Apple's green issue manager fits well within a culture built around cross-functional lines. And GSD&M's "organic" approach demonstrates how industries that have never had to deal with the environment issues can capitalize on an employee's talent and evolve an official position for dealing with them successfully.

In the next and final section of this chapter, we'll further explore how any company can harness its employees to complement established environmental programs and launch new initiatives in areas that may or may not be addressed by existing mechanisms.

HARNESSING GRASS-ROOTS ENERGY— GREEN TEAMS

Any company that ignores the enthusiastic environmental awareness that employees bring to work with them each day is missing a significant opportunity. In general, employees are eager to extend the environmental consciousness they've developed at home into their workplaces. They want their companies to solve major pollution problems. And they want to work for companies that eliminate waste through recycling programs, provide opportunities for them to help solve pollution problems, and take extensive action to reduce environmental health hazards (see Chapter 4 for specific issues relating the "Organic Office").

One of the best ways to tap the energy of your employees is to create "green teams" that search for opportunities to cut waste and eliminate pollution. In some cases, management organizes green teams to share information. At Gillette, for example, factory teams consisting of engineers and plant workers focus on ways to cut energy costs. Management then takes an active role in ensuring that the information is shared with other Gillette factories through specially designed communication channels.

In other cases, employees themselves begin looking for simple ways to create environmentally responsible workplaces. This often starts with a desire to recycle paper or aluminum cans, purchase recycled paper goods, or recycle laser toner cartridges. Informal green teams note areas where environmental improvements can be made and then pass them along to management. If management is receptive, the company will put forth the resources necessary and translate the green teams' recommendations into policy.

Ace Hardware Corporation provides an excellent case study in how green teams can bring environmental issues to the forefront. Ace's green team came into being when top management suggested that an employee start an ad hoc investigation into the feasibility of recycling. This lead to a more formalized effort that eventually reflected an overall corporate approach to the problem.

The Ace Experience

Ace's introduction to green teams actually began in a cafeteria in 1988. Employees at the Oak Brook, Illinois, headquarters had long complained about the poor quality of the food until Roger Peterson, president of the company, asked George Harris, manager of property and security, to assemble an employee group to look into the matter. The committee quickly found a new caterer with better menus, better food, and better service. Within two weeks the cafeteria ceased to be a sore spot; in fact, employees began looking forward to their lunches.

Peterson noted Harris's success and suggested that he take the same ad hoc committee approach to start a recyling program at the headquarters building. Harris quickly assembled a group representing each department in the company. Because no funds had yet been allocated to the recycling project, the committee approached one of its larger suppliers, Rubbermaid, about contributing recyling bins to the effort. Rubbermaid agreed, recognizing the opportunity to increase its products' visibility at the heart of a major purchasing center, and within a few weeks tubs in a variety of colors materialized in Ace's cafeteria (which was now bustling with patrons) for display. The idea was to let people choose which color they'd like to have in their area. At the same time, Ace's in-house print shop created stickers for the bins as well as posters announcing the impending new program. To formally kick off the recycling effort, the company sponsored an outdoor luncheon for all 800 employees of the headquarters building. Roger Peterson spoke about the importance of recycling and how many tons of paper could be saved. Next to Peterson stood a pallet of paper weighing one ton—just to ground people in reality.

As paper recycling became a way of life at Ace, the company gradually incorporated aluminum into the recycling program and then began focusing on energy conservation. Eventually, environmental awareness permeated all divisions of the company, and in 1990 Ace's executives began looking into the merchandising of environmentally responsible products. About the same time, top management made a formal strategic commitment to the environment, and Executive Vice-President David Hodnick authorized both the development of a corporate environmental marketing plan and the formation of a green team that would include representatives from all departments and regional distribution centers.

The green team's initial task was to develop a program that would coordinate all environmental efforts at Ace and monitor their progress. With the assistance of Sally Randel's Environmental Services, Inc., a Boulder-based consulting firm, the team developed this seven-point program:

1. Internal planning (refinement of the corporate recycling programs; recycling all materials from company-sponsored trade shows).

2. A survey of manufacturers designed to assess the environmental soundness of their products. The survey checks for undesirable packaging, toxicity of end product and manufacturing processes, biodegradability, and efforts to reduce waste at production level.

3. Ongoing advertising efforts to highlight environmental activities of the corporation and its co-op members.

4. An awards and recognition program to acknowledge suppliers who produce environmentally sound products.

5. A campaign to publicize Ace's environmental activities, coordinated through the corporate communications program.

6. Conducting public relations at the dealer level. This entails developing point-of-purchase materials for displaying environmentally sound wares and educational pamphlets.

7. Development a new environmental logo to be used on literature and ad slicks.

One of the immediate results of the program was a revamping of production process at Ace's Paint Division, the only manufacturing wing of the company. The effort, spear-headed by Tom Daley, head of that division, focused initially on the solvent wastes from the manufacturing process. Rather than continuing to dispose of the solvents through a licensed hazardous waste firm, Ace modified its system so that the solvents can be reclaimed and used to wash the processing tanks. Not only does the modification save the company money on the disposal of 72,000 gallons of solvent per year, but it also led to the development of an entirely new product—Ace can now distill paint sediments from the solvent wash and incorporate them into a popular metal primer.

The next phase of the "greening" of Ace's paint manufac-turing operation will entail the development of latex paints without the substances that curently render them household hazardous wastes.

And for the future? As a key player in the burgeoning do-it-yourself home improvement market, Ace realizes that nu-merous issues still need to be addressed; a typical hardware store contains as many as 3,000 items considered hazardous. Packaging will also be an ongoing issue because the days when customers buy bolts out of a barrel are over, and bubble-pack-aged rack displays are becoming the norm. In addition, be-cause customers turn to Ace for solutions to various household problems, the company is attempting to position itself as a major educator as well as a household supplier.

ENVIRONMENTAL EMPOWERMENT

Ace's success with environmental issues demonstrates the im-portance of listening to employees and empowering them to rethink the way they do their jobs. In manufacturing, a cur-rent trend is to encourage employees to sample products fre-quently and shut down equipment if bad products are coming out the hopper, rather than having them wait until 1,000 or so pieces have been made before sampling the batch and then discovering that all are defective. The same principle can be applied to other jobs; if people are allowed to briefly "stop the assembly line" to consider the environmental impact of their work, the temporary shutdown will pay off downline.

For example, rather than simply tossing out laser toner cartridges, an administrative assistant's time would be well-spent exploring remanufacturing options (see Chapter 4). Similarly, a security guard might be assigned the task of locating lights unnecessarily left on in the evening. Purchasing agents and buyers could be researching sources for recycled office supplies. And building managers could be urged to spend time figuring out what *really* goes into the company's dumpsters.

Finally, consider encouraging employees to step outside their job descriptions and spheres of responsibility. A volunteer team at Xerox Corporation's Oklahoma City plant, for example, was encouraged to work with researchers from Oklahoma State University to develop a pilot program for using toner wastes in premium asphalt products. Experiments subsequently revealed that the used toner adds elasticity and maintains the road color longer than conventional asphalt mixtures. And it puts toner that might otherwise tie up valuable landfill space to good use.

THE ENVIRONMENTAL ROLE MODEL

1. Develop a culturally appropriate organizational structure for addressing environmental issues that is clearly defined in the corporate hierarchy.

2. Include mechanisms for reporting on environmental performance for all groups in the company.

3. Build communication channels for disseminating environmental information and providing support and technical assistance at all levels.

4. Foster an atmosphere that encourages sharing of ideas and recognizes innovations.

5. Don't squander talent. Take advantage of the interests and energies of people at all levels of the company by integrating formal programs with grassroots efforts.

6. Look outward. Chapter 7 describes how people charged with improving environmental performance can benefit from working with community, business, and activist groups outside your organization.

CHAPTER 4

THE ORGANIC OFFICE
Creating an Environmentally
Sound Workplace

"Earl torments me to do the right thing. He wants me to have an environment for him and his children they will be able to live in," complained a parent to a newspaper reporter from the *New York Times.*

Earl is only a youngster. But someday Earl and his friends will be working for companies like yours. And the Earls of the world will expect you to conduct business in an environmentally responsible manner—otherwise they'll drive *you* nuts (or seek employment elsewhere).

But there's no need to wait until Earl applies for a job before you begin taking action inside your company's four walls. Many of today's workers are already looking for opportunities to bring the environmental awareness and practices they've developed at home to their jobs. Many have read popular

71

books telling them how to live more environmentally responsible lives. And most receive an annual supplementary green education from newscasts and newspaper articles centering around Earth Day.

It not only makes good sense from an employee PR perspective to make legitimate efforts to create an "organic office," but you'll also save money, build a more productive workforce, and possibly even reduce your exposure to lawsuits arising from "Sick Building Syndrome" and related issues. And consider the advice of Ciba-Geigy's Senior Vice-President, Joseph T. Sullivan: "You have to walk the way you talk." You can't possibly have a positive impact on the environment if you don't have your own house in order.

This chapter provides a topical review of the major workplace environmental issues that should be of concern to any company today. Following it will not only help your business be perceived as a "good planetary citizen," but in the long run you'll also save money and resources.

Consider incorporating the information presented in this chapter into a workplace policy that becomes part of your overall environmental strategy. Such a policy will round out your larger environmental goals and in a sense "close the loop." You might also use the information to create an internal environmental "audit"—your employees will appreciate your effort to make *their* immediate workplace more responsible. Besides, by promoting an organic office, you'll be giving every employee an opportunity to participate directly in your company's environmental efforts. As an added benefit, the resulting spirit of cooperation and teamwork will likely spill over into other company-wide endeavors.

In general, the opportunities for improving the environmental quality of a workplace fall into three categories: reducing waste, curbing pollution, and eliminating environmental health hazards. These categories not only represent opportunities for taking tangible action with quick paybacks but also cover all of the areas of concern to your employees. Each of these areas is discussed below.

WASTE REDUCTION

Few people today would argue with the fact that we are in the midst of a garbage crisis; according to the U.S. Environmental Protection Agency (EPA), more than half of the nation's landfills will be closed by 1995. Businesses can take a leadership role by providing employees the wherewithal to curb waste through recycling and by educating them about simple ways to conserve valuable resources.

A good place for any company to begin addressing waste reduction is the paper recycling bin. Next, work on reducing the actual amount of wastepaper created. Finally, look for other opportunities for waste reduction in your office.

Institute a Paper Recycling Program

U.S. corporations generate about eight million tons of paper waste each year. Much of that paper could have been recycled, and a lot of it never needed to be used in the first place. Virtually all of your fine writing, computer, and xerographic paper can be recycled—for a profit. In addition to saving the fees for trash hauling, which may run over $150 per ton in many areas, you can expect to be paid $20–40 per ton for high-grade paper. Those numbers translated into significant savings and revenues for AT&T (in 1992, AT&T recycled 62 million pounds of paper). Although the opportunities for paper recycling will vary at each company, the general principles for setting up a recycling program are the same. Here are the steps your people should take.

1. **Establish goals.** Is your company just trying to reduce trash hauling costs, or do you want to maximize your profits? If the former is your goal, you won't need an elaborate program—a box or bin in the back of each office will do. If you're trying to make money, you'll need to separate the high-quality writing paper from lower-grade copier paper—some highly motivated companies sort as many as three or more different types of paper. The more sorting, the more employee education and motivation will be required. And if people have to learn how to recognize and sort numerous intermediate grades, the recycling program may fail. As a general rule, start off with a two-sort system (high- and low-grade papers), then increase the complexity of the system if you can achieve the necessary compliance levels.

2. **Consult with a wastepaper dealer.** Select a company that has experience setting up office recycling programs. Explain your recycling goals so your contractor will best know how to service your company. Find out what you'll need in the way of bins, barrels, and so on. Many paper recycling companies can supply you with everything you need.

3. **Appoint a recycling coordinator.** This is a key step—you'll need a "torchbearer" who's personally committed to the recycling cause and can become the office expert. This coordinator job does not have to be a new position on the organizational chart; rather, it should be folded into someone's job description. For example, Cheryl La Perna at AT&T first became involved with recycling as part of her supervisory position at the loading dock, where she was responsible for waste hauling. Although

she still has other responsibilities, her involvement in AT&T's recycling program has grown significantly. Today, it's not unusual to find Cheryl traveling to various AT&T sites to promote and explain the recycling program. She also meets with recyclers to ensure that they are handling AT&T's proprietary materials appropriately.

Finally, encourage the formation of an interdepartmental committee that will work with the coordinator. To achieve maximum compliance, each department must feel a sense of ownership in the program.

4. **Spend the time necessary to educate employees.** A recycling program can only succeed if everyone understands how it works (an elaborate sorting system at one firm was undermined by an uninformed janitorial crew that combined several weeks' worth of carefully sorted paper into large plastic trash bags). An interdepartmental committee can be very helpful in this regard by taking responsibility for distributing information about goals and practices.

5. **Promote the program and provide feedback.** Success breeds success—post information on how well the program is doing in terms of pounds of paper collected, money saved, money earned, and so on. Perhaps you could even invest some of the monies saved and earned into causes that will make people proud, such as donations to environmental organizations or community environmental efforts.

Once you have a paper recyling program established, consider extending the program to other materials—aluminum, plastic, and glass. Although the paybacks will not be nearly as great (or amount to anything at all), the same people who are collecting your paper may remove other recyclables as well, thus saving the hauling costs. In any case, an aggressive recycling coordinator will research the matter, report the findings, and make a proposal that upper management can evaluate.

Finally, authorize and encourage the purchase of recycled paper goods. The quality of recycled paper products is comparable to that of virgin paper goods. And although the costs of some grades of recycled paper may be marginally higher, this is often not the case. Forward-thinking companies (as well as many government agencies) are authorizing up to a 10 percent premium for the cost of recycled paper products, with the understanding that increased demand for recycled paper will equalize costs and improve long-term opportunities for office recyling programs, while at the same time enhancing their image both with employees and customers.

Encourage a Reduction in Paper Use

In addition to supporting paper recycling throughout your organization, it is important to make everyone aware of the potential savings that can be achieved by rethinking how they use paper in their daily work. The amount of wastepaper generated by a typical office is staggering—by the end of the day, an average trash can contains hundreds of square feet of paper. The flip side of the coin is that through judicious use and reuse, every employee in your company can drastically curb the waste and save money.

For example, many tons of paper can be saved if people use the old "routing slip method" when appropriate, thinking twice before making photocopies. A staggering 37 percent of the estimated 350 billion copies made by U.S. businesses each year end up in the trash can. Encourage people to use the backs of discarded sheets of paper to make photocopies of documents not earmarked for the public (internal forms, first drafts of reports, memos, and so on) and to use the backs of paper to make phone message and note pads. Making maximum use of E-mail is also a good way to cut unnecessary paper use.

The preceding list of paper-saving ideas might seem very simple, almost trite. In fact, the ideas *are* simple. But they're also effective; if your office and department managers develop a set of guidelines based on easy-to-do procedures, you'll save resources and money. Also, because the ideas are so simple, anyone who does them will instantly feel that he or she is part of the company's effort to operate in a more environmentally responsible fashion.

Foster a Company-Wide Waste Reduction Mentality

In addition to recycling paper and other materials, supporting the recycling economy, and reducing paper usage, your company can take a number of simple steps to reduce its solid waste burden. The following actions will pay off both at the landfill and on your bottom line:

1. **Recycle or reclaim laser toner cartridges.** Laser printers offer many advantages to your office, but they pose an undue burden on landfills. Each cartridge is a bulky plastic "casket" that will sit for many years in landfills, entombing a number of plastic and metal parts. According to some environmentalists, toner cartridges are the "business equivalent of the disposable diaper." The marketing research firm BIS Strategic Decisions estimates that nearly 16 million laser toner cartridges were consumed in the United States and that, in 1992, the number jumped to 20.5 million. BIS expects users in the United States to consume 26 million cartridges in 1994 and as many as 36 million in 1997.

77

Every company should be aware of two options: remanufacturing and reclamation (options vary by cartridge brand.) A remanufactured cartridge uses the original casing and any working parts—the imaging drum and toner supply are replaced. (Note: Today's toner remanufacturers are a far cut above the original "driller and fillers" who gave toner recharging a bad reputation.)

Some toner cartridge makers, such as Canon and Hewlett Packard, offer reclamation programs through which they pay for the shipping of used cartridges back to a manufacturing facility. The cartridges are cannibalized, and many of the parts find their way into new cartridges. The manufacturers lower their production costs (and win environmental kudos), and you keep cartridges out of landfills while reducing your trash hauling costs. (As an added gesture of environmental concern, Canon and HP each make a donation of 50 cents to the Nature Conservancy and 50 cents to the National Wildlife Federation for each cartridge they receive.)

2. **Re-ink ribbons.** Although laser printers are in the limelight these days, dot matrix printers continue to sell briskly. And each year, U.S. companies use more than 100 million dot matrix ribbons, most of which wind up in landfills after a single use. As with laser toner cartridges, the one-shot use and disposal of nylon dot matrix ribbons represents a tremendous disposal problem—the ribbons will sit in their plastic casings for hundreds of years, an absolutely unnecessary waste. Just as new life can be pressed into old laser toner cartridge parts, a nylon dot matrix ribbon can be re-inked about 100 times before the ribbon fibers can no longer absorb ink.

By purchasing an inexpensive re-inking device, your company can reduce the cost of nylon ribbons by as much as a hundredfold, dropping the cost of a $10 ribbon to a dime. This can amount to substantial savings in a large company; one study estimated that the U.S. Postal Service could save as much as $5 million a year by reinking its ribbons.

3. **Provide alternatives for hard cups.** For many people today, Styrofoam is the prime example of an environmentally harmful material, because of the ozone-eating CFCs created during its production and also because of its remarkable ability to endure the elements. In a show of good environmental faith, many companies' cafeterias now offer employees the option of purchasing a reusable mug, which then qualifies them for a discount on coffee purchased for use with that mug. (At AT&T's headquarters, for example, employees can buy a mug for two dollars and then purchase coffee for 80 cents rather than the usual one dollar per cup. The mug is also substantially larger than the available Styrofoam take-outs.)

4. **Eliminate unnecessary magazine/newspaper subscriptions.** Does everyone need their own copy of every magazine that comes into your mailroom? Tons of paper can be saved if people share subscriptions whenever possible.

5. **Encourage employees to report multiple direct mail solicitations to the Direct Mail Marketing Association (DMMA).** Many of the people in your company probably receive two, three, or more solicitations from the same vendor and for the same product or service. The difference in the mailing labels may be a period, a space, or a computer foul-up ("Well, Mr. Northeastern Productions. . . ."). This not only represents a significant waste of paper (because most will wind up in the trash anyway), but it also increases the burden on your mail room. Have each department make up a form that employees can send to the DMMA with all the various ways their names appear on mailing labels. The Association will make an effort to remove the redundancies.

79

6. Insist on regular maintenance of company vehicles.
Engines in need of tune-ups or with underinflated tires can
decrease your vehicles' mileage by as much as 20 percent.

OFFICE POLLUTION REDUCTION

The word *pollution* generally conjures up images of belching
smokestacks or leaking barrels. In fact, many of the products
used in offices contain substances that should not be included
with the regular paper trash or, in the case of cleaning supplies, flushed down the drain, because they are environmental
contaminants. Your employees are becoming familiar with
them through the popular press. Here are the main product
areas that should be on your checklist:

1. **Cleaners.** No products have come under fire as much
as cleaning substances. Most commercial cleaning agents—
especially those used by janitorial crews—contain a long list
of substances ranging from formaldehyde to phenols, which
have proven health effects. More and more of your employees
are buying environmentally sound cleaning products for their
homes, and they don't want to encounter what they perceive
to be a chemical feast at work. Whether or not you personally
agree with this position, it's easy enough to request that your
maintenance staff use cleaning agents with a solid environmental rating.

2. **Office supplies.** Like cleaning supplies, some office
products are under the gun for containing substances harmful
to people and the environment. Rubber cement, for example,
contains benzene, and many graphic arts supplies contain hazardous substances. Even certain types of markers contain compounds that have been deemed undesirable. Environmentally
sound alternatives are available in each product area, and

many national office supply vendors have begun featuring them in their stores and catalogues.

3. **Paper products.** Earlier, we discussed paper recycling and the purchase of recycled paper products. A related issue is that of purchasing unbleached paper products (towels, cafeteria napkins, coffee filters, toilet paper, and so on). Chlorine bleaching, which gives paper a sparkling white appearance, creates highly toxic dioxins. Although it is debatable whether humans can be affected by dioxins in paper, there is no question that the bleaching process causes dioxin pollution at paper mills. Again, if employees are purchasing environmentally responsible paper products for their homes, don't make them compromise their values at work.

4. **Batteries.** Most office equipment operates on AC current, but some batteries are used in calculators and tape recorders. When possible, provide rechargeables. Also, provide a means of disposal separate from the regular trash.

Finally, one other area warrants discussion: printing inks. Whether your company has in-house printing services or contracts with outside vendors, the type of inks used on the presses has a significant environmental bearing. The issue concerns volatile organic compounds (VOCs), which are a significant source of ozone pollution (that is, smog). The VOCs are emitted from the petroleum-based oils that make up about 35 percent of most printer's inks and are part of the "vehicle" that carries the ink to the paper. By the time the ink dries, the VOCs have evaporated; they cannot be captured or contained, like vapors from gasoline pumps.

As an alternative, many printers are turning to vegetable oil–based inks. Inks based on soybean oil are becoming increasingly popular. Vegetable oil–based inks are available through normal distribution channels and will work on existing equipment, although some adjustments may be needed.

A related issue concerns the use of "dampening solutions" that contain isopropyl alcohol, another VOC. The solution is spread in a thin coat over the paper and acts as a moistening agent. Environmentally progressive printers have been able to modify their procedures to entirely eliminate the use of alcohol.

A complete office environmental checklist will include contracting with printers who use recycled paper stock. Some printers claim to have had bad experiences with recycled stock—an impression based on the poor quality of earlier varieties. In fact, recycled paper is now as reliable in any application as paper from virgin stock.

ENVIRONMENTAL HEALTH THREAT REDUCTION

The third consideration in creating an environmentally responsible workplace concerns identifying and eliminating or reducing indoor air pollution, an umbrella term for a variety of medical complaints arising from exposure to chemicals or microorganisms in enclosed buildings. Whereas the Occupational Safety and Health Administration has defined numerous job safety rules, most of the standards regarding this problem are based on manufacturing environments, where exposure duration is limited by job-specific ventilation systems. Moreover, indoor air pollution is a newly recognized phenomena, and there is much debate among scientists about the roles of specific pollutants. Still, indoor air pollution is likely to become one of the major issues of the next decade. Employees assume that at the very least their places of work will be safe; now, evidence suggests that the air in many commercial buildings is unhealthy.

The press is replete with stories about the large numbers of people who feel nauseated or experience headaches, stinging mucous membranes, and other ill effects after a major renovation or moving to new office quarters. These symptoms are most likely to be experienced in energy-efficient buildings with sealed windows and are therefore often referred to as Tight Building Syndrome or Sick Building Syndrome (SBS). Because this latter term is the one most commonly used in the media, we'll use it for the duration of this chapter to refer to the full range of medical problems encountered in modern or renovated office buildings.

In the past, many SBS-like complaints were written off as psychosomatic or the creations of chronic malingerers. Today, however, no company can afford to ignore the medical and scientific data demonstrating that Sick Building Syndrome is a major threat to the health of millions of workers. The EPA estimates that more than a million commercial buildings today have unhealthy air, and the World Health Organization (WHO) believes that 30 percent of all energy-efficient buildings will cause occupants to suffer SBS complaints. Moreover, some experts have estimated that the losses from absenteeism and reduced productivity caused by SBS could total in the billions of dollars each year (independent of direct medical costs).

According to Dr. Peter Sierck, an internationally recognized expert on indoor air pollution and founder of Environmental Testing and Technology, Inc., part of the difficulty in pinpointing SBS problems is that different people react differently to environmental pollutants and microorganisms; what might cause a serious reaction or illness in one person may not cause any noticeable reaction in another. Still, by recognizing the general signs and symptoms of SBS and knowing the potential causes, it is possible to solve current problems and eliminate future ones.

Causes of Sick Building Syndrome

Environmental engineer Donald Elmendorf, president of Elmendorf Environmental, Inc., points to the following as the primary factors involved in this problem:

1. **Insufficient fresh air intake.** As an energy conservation technique, most buildings recirculate the air used for heating and cooling. Although this may be a plus for energy efficiency, it is a leading cause of indoor air pollution. According to the National Institute for Occupational Safety and Health (NIOSH), more than 50 percent of indoor air problems stem directly from inadequate fresh air intake. In fact, air flow in a building may actually be more important than the presence of contaminants.

2. **Poor maintenance of a building's Heating/Ventilation/Air Conditioning (HVAC) System.** An improperly maintained HVAC system can be a fertile breeding ground for microbiological contaminants that can spread throughout an entire building. The initial outbreak of Legionnaires' Disease is the most well known example of this problem.

3. **Water damage.** Whenever a tightly sealed building experiences excessive moisture from broken pipes or malfunctioning sprinkler systems there is a risk of accelerated growth of molds and bacteria. Whether the growth occurs in the HVAC system, inside walls, or on carpeting, it can infect large groups of people if the building is tightly sealed or has inadequate ventilation.

4. **Emissions from office equipment.** Laser printers and copiers as well as thermal machines like blueprint copiers can all contribute to indoor air pollution. Laser printers and personal copiers, for example, emit ozone. If the employees feed

the wrong kind of labels or envelopes through a laser printer, toxic gases may be emitted.

5. **Offgassing from building materials.** Many new building materials contain substances, such as formaldehyde, that "offgas" and make their way into the ventilation system. The EPA has identified more than 500 different organic compounds that typically occur at high enough concentrations to be a health problem, particularly in airtight buildings. Carpeting and carpeting adhesives, paints, glues, caulking, and composite building materials often contain volatile compounds that can cause adverse effects in sensitive people. The fabric on partitions is also sometimes problematic—the fibers in the materials may absorb pollutants and then release them into the ventilation system.

6. **Changes in building use or layout.** Medical complaints often arise after a building renovation. This may be due to the fact that more people are using the space than the ventilation system can handle. Also, adding walls or partitions can disrupt or completely cut off the fresh air supply.

7. **Cleaning methods and materials.** Office cleaning materials contain numerous pollutants that can contribute to Sick Building Syndrome. If the residues from these materials aren't rinsed thoroughly, they will end up in the air pumped through the building.

8. **Use of pesticides.** Indoor application of pesticides can pollute the air, especially after repeated use.

Curing Sick Building Syndrome

As dire as Sick Building Syndrome may sound, the diagnosis and cures are sometimes relatively inexpensive and simple. In addition to helping pinpoint the sources of the problem, the steps suggested below can establish indoor air quality maintenance as an ongoing routine rather than a remedial or emergency activity.

1. **Sanction an indoor environmental audit.** An audit is the first step. A qualified environmental firm will point out areas that need attention, such as HVAC filters that need cleaning or air conditioning system drip pans.

2. **Eliminate pollution from office equipment.** Laser printers and copiers, which generate ozone as a part of normal operations, all have ozone filters. Most people forget that these need to be maintained. Rearranging office equipment can also help; in poorly ventilated, small spaces, even well-maintained office equipment may generate enough ozone to cause problems for people sensitive to the gas.

3. **Reduce indoor pollution from chemicals.** Problems caused by cleaning solvents entering the ventilation system are easily remedied by switching to products that do not contain the offending agents. Care should also be taken when chemicals are used in laboratories and engineering shops adjacent to office space.

4. **Take prompt remedial action when needed.** In some cases more complex actions need to be taken to improve ventilation or rid buildings of mold, fungi, or microorganisms— especially after water damage or improper carpet cleaning. With the help of a qualified environmental engineer, you can identify these problems and respond to them before they have an adverse effect on the health and performance of your employees.

5. **Try some real greenery.** Finally, some experts are recommending the use of plants to remove toxic substances from the air. NASA experiments have revealed that philodendrons

actually thrive on compounds that make humans ill, like form-aldehyde. English ivy can process benzene (a solvent and known carcinogen), and chrysanthemums appear to enjoy tri-chloroethylenes (also a carcinogen which, until recently, was commonly used in various office products).

VDT Radiation

Some experts include video display terminal (VDT) radiation in the general category of indoor air pollution, so we'll briefly describe the status of the issue. Few issues have sparked as much debate as that of VDT radiation, which actually consists of two types of emissions: extremely low frequency (ELF) and very low frequency (VLF). Until recently no one suspected that either type posed a biological problem. As a result, monitor makers did not bother to shield the electromagnetic coils re-sponsible for the emissions. Now, however, numerous scientists contend that ELF and VLF may be harmful to human beings.

While the jury is still out on the subject, your company can issue the following guidelines. If the claims about VDT turn out to be warranted, you'll be ahead of the game; if false, you won't have wasted much effort.

1. **Educate employees.** Encourage employees to maintain at least 28 inches between themselves and their monitors—the emissions fall off significantly at that distance.

2. **Utilize safer office furniture layouts.** Rearrange the positions of monitors so that no one's head is bumping an-other person's monitor. The emissions from the backs and sides are significantly greater than from the front, due to the position of the offending electronic equipment in the monitor. ELF and VDT radiation fall off dramatically at four feet and are very weak at ten feet from the back or sides of a monitor.

3. **Suggest "VDT breaks."** Most people leave their computers on during the course of the day. Although it's true that leaving a computer on for long periods of time is easier on the electronics, monitors can be turned on and off without jeopardizing their circuitry.

4. **Upgrade equipment.** As you purchase new systems or replace old monitors, select models that meet the MPR II standards for video display terminal radiation. An increasing number of manufacturers are offering low-emission monitors that cost no more than their conventional counterparts.

At the very least, your employees will appreciate your efforts to provide guidelines and safe equipment. And who knows, you just might be taking positive action that will help preserve the health of your most vital assets.

FIVE SIMPLE WAYS TO IMPROVE YOUR COMPANY'S ENVIRONMENT

1. Encourage company-wide recycling of all resources; appoint coordinators to ensure that the recycling efforts succeed. Provide feedback and support.

2. Foster a "tightwad" culture in which people naturally find ways to get the most out of every sheet of paper and press spent materials back into service.

3. Keep your office "green"; advocate the purchase of environmentally friendly products.

4. Don't wait for the final word on indoor air pollution; be on the cutting edge for the sake of your employees and your reputation as an environmental leader.

5. Walk like you talk; apply your environmental mission statement to every mundane aspect of your company.

CHAPTER 5

THE TEN LAWS
OF ECO-MARKETING
*Marketing and Advertising in the
Environmental Age*

"Talk about nerve. Talk about shamelessness. Talk about Chutzpah. For the past three decades, General Motors Corporation has put on the full court press in Congress, the administration and legislatures across the country to prevent, dilute and slow down governmental clean-air action. Now, with eco-sanity finally coming to the fore and federal regulation at last getting teeth, suddenly GM, via N W Ayer, New York, is saluting '20 years of environmental progress.' Oh please. This is like John Wayne Gacy celebrating the International Year of the Child. Zero Stars."

Zero stars for GM—sounds like a rating conferred by an activist organization, doesn't it? In fact, that's how *Advertising Age* rated a full-page General Motors ad resplendent with a dazzling color photograph of scenic mountain wilderness and a headline proclaiming, "Earth Day 1990: General Motors Marks 20 Years of Environmental Progress." The article went on to lambaste other companies for taking advantage of the ecological movement through distortions and sins of omission in their advertising. (Interestingly, GM seems to have learned a few lessons about making good on its intent to be environmentally responsible; in June 1992 the company struck up a pact with one of its most vocal opponents, the Environmental Defense Fund (EDF). The two will work together to develop models and standards that automakers can deploy to reduce pollution during various manufacturing processes.)

General Motors is not the first company to underestimate the knowledge of the consuming public, the media, and environmental critics—nor will it be the last. Companies that wish to tout the environmental qualities of their products and services will have to back up their claims with hard facts. (They'll also have to pay close attention to federal and state lawmakers who are conducting aggressive campaigns to crack down on companies that make false or dubious environmental claims—see Chapter 6.) This chapter is designed to help you position your products, services, and overall corporate image in a way that reflects their environmental worthiness without causing a backlash from consumer organizations or environmental critics.

NEW MOOD: CONSUMER WARINESS

Before considering specific dos and don'ts in eco-marketing, it's important to understand the mood of the buying public. Following Earth Day 1990, numerous polls revealed a tremendous interest on the part of consumers to buy products that are formulated and packaged with the environment in mind and to support companies that conduct themselves in an environmentally responsible manner. Then came the inevitable backlash—consumers grew skeptical of "green" claims following well-publicized marketing fiascoes such as Mobil's attempt to offer "degradable" trash bags. Also, as the economy worsened, some marketing experts began predicting that more consumers would consider traditional measures such as functionality, price, and brand name before environmental quality.

Despite predictions that environmental consuming was a passing fad, a mid-1992 *Advertising Age* poll conducted by Yankelovich Clancy Shulman revealed that consumers' interest in the environment hadn't abated. Sixty-three percent of the people surveyed were more likely to purchase a product based on its environmental qualities than they were three years ago. At the same time, 20 percent believed that the environmental claims on product labels were not very believable, 8 percent said they were not all believable, 3 percent were unsure, and 62 percent felt that the claims were "somewhat believable." Only 8 percent felt that the claims were "very believable" (3 percent were unsure). The responses to a question concerning the environmental claims in product advertising were nearly identical. Also of interest was the response to a question concerning who should regulate marketers' environmental claims. Only 11 percent said that manufacturers should be allowed to police themselves—40 percent thought that the federal government should have the role of watchdog, and another 40 percent thought that the responsibility should rest with the states (8 percent were unsure).

Clearly, both opportunity and danger await makers of everything from automobiles to consumer products. To sell goods and services to an interested—but wary—marketplace, it is critical to bear in mind that eco-marketing and eco-advertising are very different from any other type of marketing campaigns. Whatever you say, in any media format, will be scrutinized carefully by both the law and environmental watchdog groups. Also, environmental issues are unique in that every claim you make will be evaluated by people who may have conflicting facts and numbers. Regardless of who, in the end, turns out to be correct, you may well find yourself caught up in a controversy that casts doubt over your intentions and the positive environmental qualities of your products (see the Fifth Law of Eco-Marketing, discussed later in this chapter).

In short, you cannot conduct "marketing as usual" when using the environmental worthiness of a product, or the environmentally responsible actions of your company, as a marketing hook. Successful green marketing requires input from knowledgeable people throughout the company and from people who understand the emotional nature of the issues involved. Eco-marketeers should expand their "cultural media diet" to include environmental literature. Since the public primarily learns about the environment through the media, and the media in turn relies on environmental groups for information, it pays to find out what your critics believe to be environmental truths.

You also might want to assemble a review board similar to the Community Advisory Committees discussed in Chapter 7 that includes people representing grass-roots or national environmental organizations. These days it's not uncommon for formerly bitter enemies to sit at the same table—just look at the joint projects that EDF has conducted with McDonald's and General Motors. Five years ago such alliances would have been considered unimaginable.

Finally, an important prerequisite to eco-marketing is to understand that people who are willing to make lifestyle changes, even simple ones, to improve the environment in some small way feel a sense of personal satisfaction and commitment. They feel that they're doing their part and that the companies they work for and buy from should show similar efforts in reaching the common goal of a cleaner and safer environment. Consequently, when they read about corporations exploiting the environment through deceptive or misleading advertising, they become cynical and even incensed. What marketeers perceive as a waning interest in environmentally conscious consumption may therefore be skepticism, frustration, and unwillingness to support companies with dubious motives.

The good news is that it's easy to avoid the pitfalls that thrust companies into the headlines and sully relations with customers and prospects. The following Ten Laws of Eco-Marketing point out the major problem areas that can derail your efforts, regardless of your good intentions:

1. **Avoid nebulous slogans.**
2. **Don't invent "a tradition" of environmental excellence.**
3. **Watch your language.**
4. **Give the truth, the whole truth, and nothing but the truth.**
5. **Pick your numbers carefully.**
6. **Build credibility.**
7. **Be a partner, not a teacher.**
8. **Show relevance.**
9. **Don't tout the trivial.**
10. **Make eco-marketing part of a sustained effort.**

Each of the laws is described below:

1. **Avoid nebulous slogans.** Today's consumers are not likely to be swayed by image pieces with the general message, "we care about the planet." Instead, many consumers are in "action mode" and are not about to be swayed by mere talk or hollow slogans. In the post–Rio 1992 summit days, the debate has shifted from discussion of the nature and extent of our environmental problems to specific talk about how we're going to solve them. No one will be impressed by your intentions to become part of the solution. Be specific or be silent.

2. **Don't invent "a tradition" of environmental excellence.** You can't rewrite or reinterpret history to paint your company as an environmental hero. Perhaps your founder's family did actually live in a log cabin and avoid waste like the plague. Perhaps your products never did contain environmentally damaging agents. Or perhaps your CEO's family has long enjoyed fishing or the wildlife. The point is, people care about what you're doing *today*.

A related issue concerns past environmental performance. A few of the problems with GM's "20 Years of Environmental Progress" ad are the company's previously hostile position to environmental legislation, its position with regards to mass transit, and the fact that it makes a product both directly and indirectly responsible for widespread pollution. The public and environmental critics will acknowledge positive action in the future but won't simply erase bad memories because the company has announced an "about face" with regards to the environment.

3. **Watch your language.** Terminology represents one of the biggest mine fields for eco-marketers. An increasing number of states are developing strict definitions and guidelines

for terms such as "recycled" and "recyclable" (as we'll see later in this chapter), and the federal government has issued its own set of guidlines for national standards. In addition to keeping abreast of the laws, be wary of using terms such as "earth-friendly" and "environmentally friendly"—using them may provoke immediate suspicion on the part of consumers.

4. Give the truth, the whole truth, and nothing but the truth. In the Environmental Age, truths that need to be qualified with footnotes won't cut it. Procter & Gamble discovered this in 1990 when it ran ads for its Pampers and Luvs brand disposable diapers touting a new composting program, designed to solve a nagging problem that has made disposable diapers one of the most highly criticized consumer products in history. (See Chapter 8.) One P&G ad included a photograph of an unplanted tree with the headline, "This baby is growing up in disposable diapers." Although the concept is intriguing and offers an innovative solution to a serious problem, the ads were, in effect, premature; at the time they were run, municipal solid waste composting was available in only ten pilot cities, meaning that the majority of the diapers Procter & Gamble sold would have made their way into landfills. A footnote to the ad mentioning that only ten municipal programs were in place just served to raise the ire of critics of disposable diapers in general. (See Chapter 8 for more details.)

5. Pick your numbers carefully. Whereas buyers of analgesics might be convinced, or at least not offended by, claims such as "Three out of four doctors . . . ," be prepared to support every claim you make and to run into well-documented counterevidence. Unfortunately, not all scientific data related to environmental problems is unequivocal. It's possible, for example, to construct equally powerful arguments for the use of paper and plastic bags. Critics of pesticides argue for non-chemical or natural approaches to pest management; those on the opposing side argue that such approaches are ineffective and that turning away from chemical pest controls will eventually result in widespread famines in developing countries. Scientists argue among themselves about the dangers posed by various levels of environmental contaminants, the extent and significance of the ozone hole, and the threat posed by toxic waste dumps.

The point is that when it comes to the environment, people often believe what they want to believe, especially if the numbers support a favored position. Compare your facts and figures to those in the popular and environmental press. Remember, even if your own data or data supplied by a trade association disagrees with the facts and figures cited in a popular book or publication, the consuming public turns to the media for information about the environment. If your numbers or facts are out of sync with those commonly cited in the press, then find a resolution before using them in a marketing or advertising campaign.

6. **Build credibility.** If the key to the restaurant business is location, location, and location, then the key to successful eco-marketing is credibility, credibility, and credibility. Given the skepticism of today's consumer and environmental watchdog groups, consider bringing in third parties to substantiate your claims and shore up confidence that your efforts are sincere and based on valid environmental science. (See Chapter 9 for a description of the criteria that various organizations apply when they evaluate a company's environmental worthiness; also, Chapter 7 discusses numerous opportunities for strategic alliances with community groups and environmental organizations.)

7. **Be a partner, not a teacher.** This law is a corollary to the one preceding. It also flies in the face of one of the major marketing trends of the 90s: consumer education. If you're

in the international airline business, your customers may well appreciate learning about how to conduct themselves in foreign markets (Northwest Airlines, for example, has done a splendid job of providing information about business etiquette and cultural pitfalls). But if you're promoting new solutions to thorny environmental problems, the public (and legions of experts) probably have ideas of their own about the subject. If you present yourself as an authority on anything but the most basic concepts, *someone* out there will be ready to attack your position. You also run the risk of being accused of bias in reporting your side of the story in order to "greenwash" your performance. If you have a meaningful environmental story to tell, join forces with environmental, civic, or municipal organizations to get your information communicated to a national audience (see Chapter 7 on how to form working alliances). The next chapter has suggestions on working with the media and sponsoring a national dialogue on issues that affect the way you do business.

8. **Show relevance.** At the same time that *Advertising Age* slammed General Motors, it awarded the makers of WD-40 $1/2$ stars for an ad with a headline that read, "Stop squeaks, prevent rust, and preserve National Parks." The ad shows photographs of two devices powered by internal combustion engines (an outboard motor and a mobile home) and describes the company's $50,000 donation to the National Park Service. Whoever created and approved the ad probably saw some relevance in the odd collection of images and ideas, but it's unlikely that the company has risen to the top of anyone's Green List.

Advertising Age also pointed out a similarly irrelevant line of thinking in an ad from Pentax that showed a photograph of the edge of the woods, a picture of a new Pentax camera, and a headline that read, "Preserve your World." Here's what the publication's critics had to say about it: "OK, preserve does have a photo-enviro double meaning. And it's always good advice, as this ad repeats, not to trash your photographic venues. But the specific connections between the Pentax IQ Zoom 60X and environmental responsibility is spurious, silly and substantially obnoxious. 1½ stars."

The moral? In the Age of Information, people are bombarded with data that competes for processing space. They simply filter out irrelevant or nonsensical information, so why waste your money?

9. Don't tout the trivial. This law of eco-marketing is probably ignored more than any of the others. It applies to the formulation and packaging of products and to announcements concerning companies' accomplishments in cleaning up the environment. After Earth Day 1990, for example, several major airlines featured ads announcing that they recycled their soda and beer cans. On a scale of one to ten, this could not have rated very high on most people's priority lists, especially when you consider the atmospheric pollution caused by jet aircraft.

One maker of solid deodorants didn't miss the opportunity to mention that its products were "earth-friendly"—no aerosol sprays. But what about the totally unrecylable plastic containers and tops? The fact that one of your products is made or packaged without an offending agent does not necessarily render it environmentally sound. If you're going to capitalize on the environmental quality of your products, apply the following litmus tests:

- Does the packaging or formulation of the product solve a widespread and recognized environmental problem (in terms of ultimate disposal, hazardous/toxic constituents during manufacturing, safety to people and the environment during use, and so on)?

- Do the products set new standards that go beyond compliance requirements? It is simply not enough to do what the law requires; companies that receive high praise for their environmental efforts will demonstrate how they exceed regulations.

In terms of corporate efforts in the environmental arena, it's just as important to narrow your focus to solid accomplishments. Consider how the makers of WD-40 touted their $50,000 donation to an environmental cause. Critics responded that this was a minuscule contribution to an effort that will require many billions of dollars (just cleaning the nation's toxic waste dumps will require upwards of $500 billion). A trivial donation hardly earns a company the right to imply that it has made a difference in preserving the environment.

Here are several questions you should consider before using your company's environmental track record as part of a marketing program:

- Are the accomplishments substantial? If they're monetary donations, measure them against real cleanup and preservation costs—you can avoid embarrassing criticisms such as the one that the makers of WD-40 experienced. If you're touting emissions performance, is it truly noteworthy? As in the case of products, simply complying with standards won't impress anyone.

- Is an environmental accomplishment part of a sustained campaign, or is it an isolated effort? (See the Tenth Law of Eco-Marketing.) The public is looking for an ongoing commitment to environmental cleanup and preservation on the part of companies—one-shot donations or feats will appear opportunistic. Also, a single act, in the face of a poor environmental track record, will do nothing

101

but raise the ire of critics—wait until you have done something demonstrating that your company is truly on its way to becoming an environmentally responsible member of the business community.

- Was the accomplishment motivated solely by environmental goals? If not, present other factors as well. When engineers at Gillette worked to reduce water consumption on a manufacturing line by over 96 percent, their initial intent was to save water—pure and simple. They eventually realized a significant financial bonus due to water usage rates increasing dramatically in the Boston area (see Chapter 8 for details). That doesn't negate the benefits of their conservation efforts, but a full accounting of the facts certainly preempted accusations of opportunistic PR. In short, Gillette scores a double win—the company saves money and the public perceives it as both conservation and bottom-line oriented.

10. **Make eco-marketing part of a sustained effort.** There's no better way to be labeled as a company that exploits the environment than to run a one-time image ad professing concern for the wilderness. A solid eco-marketing campaign recognizes the wariness of the public and the overall negative image that business must overcome. Successful eco-marketing reflects a company's overall environmental philosophy. In fact, companies should consider eco-marketing as an outgrowth of that philosophy—an opportunity to communicate their vision with the consuming public on a regular basis.

ECO-MARKETING AND THE LAW

After Earth Day 1990, the federal government and a number of Attorneys General began studying various problems with environmental marketing. In 1991 and 1992, a number of states passed laws regulating environmental claims made in advertising and labeling, and in July 1992 the Federal Trade Commission (FTC) issued its own set of guidelines. This chapter summarizes the federal guidelines as well as the guidelines developed by a task force of Attorneys General, which had a significant influence on the Federal Trade Commission's recommendations and on the labeling/advertising laws passed by various states.

Federal Guidelines

The July 1992 federal guidelines were developed in concert with the Environmental Protection Agency and the U.S. Office of Consumer Affairs and were based on input from a broad spectrum of interests including trade, consumer, environmental, and industry groups. Although the FTC guidelines are not in and of themselves legally enforceable, they serve to provide a framework for helping marketers conform with the law. The guidelines focus on the areas listed in Table 5.1.

In 1995, the FTC plans to review public comments on the guidelines before developing enforceable regulations. In the meantime, companies will have to comply with state laws, which brings us to the second half of the equation for marketers and advertisers of environmentally friendly products and services.

State Laws Regulating Environmental Claims

In the absence of any binding federal laws, product makers may well find themselves faced with the prospect of complying with a pastiche of labeling and advertising requirements and

TABLE 5.1
SUMMARY OF FTC GUIDELINES FOR ENVIRONMENTAL CLAIMS

General Environmental Benefit Claims. In general, unqualified general environmental claims are difficult to interpret, and may have a wide range of meanings to consumers. Every express and implied material claim conveyed to consumers about an objective quality should be substantiated. Unless they can be substantiated, broad environmental claims should be avoided or qualified.

Degradable, Biodegradable, Photodegradable. In general, unqualified degradability claims should be substantiated by evidence that the product will completely break down and return to nature, that is, decompose into elements found in nature within a reasonably short period of time after consumers dispose of it in the customary way. Such claims should be qualified to the extent necessary to avoid consumer deception about: (a) the product or package's ability to degrade in the environment where it is customarily disposed; and (b) the extent and rate of degradation.

Compostable. Unqualified claims should be substantiated by evidence that all of the materials in the product or package will break down into compost in a safe and timely manner in an appropriate composting program or facility, or in a home composting pile or device. Compostable claims should be qualified to the extent necessary to avoid consumer deception: (1) if municipal composting facilities are not available to a substantial majority of consumers or communities where the product is sold; (2) if the claim misleads consumers about the environmental benefit provided when the product is disposed of in a landfill; or (3) if consumers misunderstand the claim to mean that the package can be safely composted in their home compost pile or device, when in fact it cannot.

Recyclable. In general, a product or package should not be marketed as recyclable unless it can be collected, separated, or otherwise recovered from the solid waste stream for use in the form of raw materials in the manufacture or assembly of a new product or package. Unqualified recyclable claims may be made if the entire product or package, excluding incidental components, is recyclable. Claims about products with both recyclable and non-recyclable components should be adequately qualified. If incidental components significantly

104

TABLE 5.1 Continued

limit the ability to recycle product, the claim would be deceptive. If, because of its size or shape, a product is not accepted in recycling programs, it should not be marketed as recyclable. Qualification may be necessary to avoid consumer deception about the limited availability of recycling programs and collection sites if recycling collection sites are not available to a substantial majority of consumers and communities.

Recycled Content. In general, claims of recycled content should only be made for materials that have been recovered or diverted from the solid waste stream, either during the manufacturing process (preconsumer) or after consumer waste (post-consumer). An advertiser should be able to substantiate that pre-consumer content would otherwise have entered the solid waste stream. Distinctions made between pre- and post-consumer content should be substantiated. Unqualified claims may be made if the entire product or package, excluding minor, incidental components, is made from recycled material. Products or packages only partially made of recycled material should be qualified to indicate the amount, by weight, in the finished product or package.

Source Reduction. In general, claims that a product or package has been reduced or is lower in weight, volume, or toxicity should be qualified to the extent necessary to avoid consumer deception about the amount of reduction and the basis for any comparison asserted.

Refillable. In general, an unqualified refillable claim should not be asserted unless a system is provided for: (1) the collection and return of the package for refill; or (2) the later refill of the package by consumers with product subsequently sold in another package. The claim should not be made if it is up to consumers to find ways to refill the package.

Ozone Safe and Ozone Friendly. In general, a product should not be advertised as "ozone-safe," or "ozone-friendly," or as not containing CFC's if the product contains any ozone-depleting chemical. Claims about the reduction of a product's ozone-depletion potential may be made if adequately substantiated.

the attendant problems of satisfying all of them with a single marketing campaign.

A number of states have aggressively pursued companies that bandy about meaningless or misleading environmental terms. The most notable case is that of Mobil Oil and its Hefty Trashbags. The company was sued in six states for deceptive advertising and consumer fraud; because of the negative press, Mobil became what columnist John Carroll called "the Michael Milken of Green Marketing." (It's interesting to note that not being the only or even the first company to hit the market with these claims didn't protect Mobil from vilification.) The problem was one of language. Yes, the bags were degradable, provided that they were exposed to sunlight and other elements not normally present in the midst of a landfill. Mobil agreed to remove the label from its trash bag line.

Much of the action has taken place in the offices of various Attorneys General. For example, the AGs in California, Florida, Massachusetts, Minnesota, Missouri, New York, Tennessee, Texas, Utah, Washington, and Wisconsin met during 1990 and 1991 to draft "The Green Report," which provides recommendations for responsible environmental advertising. The Report covers four areas—specificity of environmental advertising claims, relevance of claims to current solid waste management options, the substantive nature of advertising claims, and the support of claims with scientific evidence. The summary recommendations are listed in Table 5.2. As you'll see, some of the language concerning the definition of terms such as "recyclable" made its way into the FTC guidelines. Other parts of the AG's recommendations are becoming incorporated into laws that have been passed or are being considered by various states.

Look for more guidelines such as those put forth in "The Green Report" making their way into law. A number of states have passed legislation that defines exactly how certain terms

TABLE 5.2
SUMMARY RECOMMENDATIONS OF THE GREEN REPORT

1. **CLAIMS SHOULD BE SPECIFIC.**
   Claims should be as specific as possible and not general, vague, incomplete or overly broad.

1.1 *Use of the Terms "Environmentally Friendly" and "Safe for the Environment."*
   Generalized environmental claims which imply that a product has no negative or adverse impact on the environment should be avoided. Instead, claims should be specific and state the precise environmental benefit that the product provides.

1.2 *Pre-existing Environmental Attributes.*
   The promotion of a previously-existing but previously-unadvertised positive environmental attribute should not create, either explicitly or implicitly, the perception that the product has been recently modified or improved.

1.3 *Removal of Harmful Ingredient.*
   In promoting the removal of a single harmful ingredient or a few harmful ingredients from a product or package, care should be taken to avoid the impression that the product is good for the environment in all respects.

1.4 *Benefits of Products versus Packaging.*
   A clear distinction should be made between the environmental attributes of a *product* and the environmental attributes of its *packaging*.

1.5 *Use of Term "Recycled."*
   Recycled content claims should be specific, and separate percentages should be disclosed for post-consumer and pre-consumer materials. To avoid the potential for deception, the Task Force recommends that only post-consumer materials be referred to as "recycled" materials. Recaptured factory material should be referred to by some other term, such as "reprocessed (or recovered) industrial material."

1.6 *Comparative Claims.*
   Only complete and full comparisons should be made; the basis for the comparison should be stated.

107

TABLE 5.2 Continued

1.7 *Product Life Assessments.*
The results of product life assessments should not be used to advertise or promote specific products until uniform methods for conducting such assessments are developed and a general consensus is reached among government, business, environmental and consumer groups on how this type of environmental comparison can be advertised non-deceptively.

1.8 *Third Party Certifications and Seals of Approval.*
Environmental certifications and seals of approval must be designed and promoted with great care, to avoid misleading the public.

1.9 *Source Reduction Claims.*
Source reduction claims should be specific, and where possible, include percentages. Comparisons should be clear and complete.

2. **CLAIMS SHOULD REFLECT CURRENT SOLID WASTE MANAGEMENT OPTIONS**.
Environmental claims relating to the disposability or potential for recovery of a particular product (e.g., "compostable" or "recyclable") should be made in a manner that clearly discloses the general availability of the advertised option where the product is sold.

2.1 *Use of the Terms "Degradable," "Biodegradable" and "Photo-degradable."*
Products that are currently disposed of primarily in landfills or through incinerations—whether paper or plastic—should not be promoted as "degradable," "biodegradable," or "photodegradable."

2.2 *Use of Term "Compostable."*
Unqualified compostability claims should not be made for products sold nationally unless a significant amount of the product is currently being composted everywhere the product is sold. In all other cases, compostability claims should be accompanied by a clear disclosure about the limited availability of this disposal option. If a claim of degradability is made in the context of a product's compostability, a disclosure should be made that the product is not designed to degrade in a landfill.

TABLE 5.2   Continued

2.3 *Use of Term "Recyclable".*
Unqualified recyclability claims should not be made for products sold nationally unless a significant amount of the product is being recycled everywhere the product is sold. Where a product is being recycled in many areas of the country, a qualified recyclability claim can be made. If consumers have little or no opportunity to recycle a product, recyclability claims should not be made.

2.4 *Safe for Disposal.*
Vague safety claims concerning disposability should be avoided. Instead, products should specifically disclose those environmentally dangerous materials or additives that have been eliminated.

3. **CLAIMS SHOULD BE SUBSTANTIVE.**
Environmental claims should be substantive.

3.1 *Trivial and Irrelevant Claims.*
Trivial and irrelevant claims should be avoided.

3.2 *Single Use Products.*
Single use disposable products promoted on the basis of environmental attributes should be promoted carefully to avoid the implication that they do not impose a burden on the environment.

4. **CLAIMS SHOULD BE SUPPORTED.**
Environmental claims should be supported by competent and reliable evidence.

may be used in advertising. California, for example, passed a "Truth in Environmental Advertising Law," which carefully defines the use of the terms *recycled, recyclable, biodegradable, ozone-friendly,* and *photodegradable.* As of this writing, Connecticut, Indiana, Maine, New York, Rhode Island, and Wisconsin have passed similar laws, and a half-dozen states have pending laws likely to make it on the books in the near future.

ECO-MARKETING REVIEWED

1. Respect the public's commitment to the environment and its desire for bona fide, positive action.

2. Understand the perceptual gulf that can exist between your understanding and the public's understanding of environmental issues. Being right does not necessarily guarantee success.

3. Treat eco-marketing as a new field with its own unique pitfalls and opportunities.

4. Don't operate in a vacuum—get input from your toughest critics.

5. Make eco-marketing an extension of your corporate culture.

6. When it comes to eco-marketing, the meek will inherit the regulations—act now while the window for participatory change is still open. Get involved in state and national dialogues to whatever extent you can through public comment, forums, and so on.

CHAPTER 6

ECO-SPEAK

*Conducting an Effective Environmental
PR Campaign*

"This is not a disaster, it is merely a change. The area won't have disappeared, it will just be under water. Where you now have cows, you will have fish." A clip from *National Lampoon*? A parody from "Saturday Night Live"? Neither. A minor government official actually uttered these words to the Bangladesh delegation at an international conference on global warming. And although no one in corporate America today would even think about trying to hoodwink anyone into believing that serious environmental problems are benefits in disguise, there is a tendency to underestimate the special needs associated with environmental PR.

As public interest in ecologically responsible living grows, fueled by Earth Days, environmental disasters, international conferences like the 1992 World Environmental Summit in

Rio de Janeiro, and other events, communication about environmental issues becomes increasingly important. Such communication appeals to an audience primed to learn more about environmentalism. It can also help a company define and establish a positive image as a leader in responsible environmental management—as long as the image is accurate.

Good environmental PR should inform your stakeholders of your company's efforts to operate in an environmentally responsible manner and of your commitment to becoming part of a large-scale solution to pressing environmental problems. It should also serve as a means for stimulating a dialogue with the surrounding community about your company's position with regards to environmental issues—what it's doing, what it plans to do, and how it can serve in the local fight against pollution. All this means giving special attention to the quality and nature of your environmental communications both to the media and your various stakeholders.

This chapter explores how to effectively publicize your company's environmental efforts without being labeled as exploitive or self-aggrandizing. It discusses opportunities and land mines that await your company as it attempts to communicate its accomplishments and plans through the media or directly to consumers, employees, and the local community. The first part covers core communications issues and defines a general philosophy that should underlie all of your public relations efforts. The second covers media releases, and the third focuses on the use of newsletters and special publications designed to be used in-house or in the marketplace. The fourth section discusses the use of special events and community outreach programs to promote public awareness of your environmental programs and your intentions to pursue a sound environmental policy. The final section offers pointers on using an outside PR agency to help communicate your message.

AN ENVIRONMENTAL COMMUNICATIONS PHILOSOPHY

Customers, employees, shareholders, community members, and others value complete, factual, and honest information on environmental subjects. Companies run into trouble when they sell one side of a controversial issue and pretend that other viewpoints do not exist, when they proclaim their commitment to the environment but do little or nothing to prove that commitment, or when they promote a highly visible, environment-conscious action while hiding an environmental embarrassment.

In a report entitled "Managing the Global Environmental Challenge," Business International identified these *Ten Communication Commandments:*

1. Be open with the public, but don't underestimate the difficulties involved. Make sure the record the company stands on is solid before claims are made.

2. For credibility's sake, be prepared to share performance achievements and weaknesses. Follow up with information on problems that are being corrected.

3. Remember that the environmental audience is made up of many segments that must be addressed individually as well as collectively.

4. Public acceptance of a less-than-perfect company is possible if the firm can demonstrate it is doing something to improve performance.

5. Encourage employees at all levels of the corporation to be "ambassadors" for the firm.

6. Take risks. Initiate dialogues with critics, and set public goals that stretch the limits of your current capabilities.

7. Help educate the public. People who have a basic understanding of scientific issues and data will be better able to interpret corporate performance fairly.

8. Be discriminating. Evaluate where there is a competitive advantage in revealing environmental successes to the public.

9. Be flexible. As the company's environmental posture changes and grows, communications choices reflect those changes.

10. Know where you stand vis-à-vis your competitors and other industries, and be willing to share your wisdom for the betterment of industry as a whole.

MEDIA RELEASES

Companies today are in a classic double-bind or "damned-if-you-do, damned-if-you-don't" position with regard to publicizing their efforts to do business in an environmentally responsible fashion. On the one hand, customers, environmental groups, and legislators are demanding evidence that corporate America is making a serious effort to improve its environmental record. On the other, corporate environmental PR is often greeted with skepticism and mistrust. The following five guidelines will help you steer clear of troubled waters:

1. **Treat environmental issues as a special topic requiring special knowledge**. Too often companies assume that environmental issues can be handled from a PR standpoint the way other corporate events are handled (for example, reports of improved earnings, product announcements, plant openings, executive personnel changes, and so on). Unfortunately, with environmental

114

issues there is great risk of a well-intentioned PR department trying to make headline news out of nonissues, such as the company achieving an emission level already mandated by regulations.

Whatever your company says will be scrutinized by extremely knowledgeable critics. The problems caused by the loose use of the term "ozone-friendly" is instructive because it points out how easy it is to make logical assumptions about the value of a particular environmental accomplishment. True, if CFCs are a major destroyer of the ozone, not having them in your product should make it more environmentally friendly. But without the knowledge that the use of CFCs had been banned several years earlier and that the substitute propellants have problems of their own, the claim becomes a liability.

The solution? Give at least one individual in your company's PR department a mandate to become an expert on environmentalism. That person should read all popular books and magazines on the subject. He or she should also become a member of the major environmental groups and read their publications very carefully. This will make it possible to avoid potential blunders—such as the CFC issue—and to venture into potentially thorny areas with the awareness of a possible backlash.

The in-house expert should also maintain a clipping file of current topics relating to the environment that appear in the media. Remember, your corporate scientists, engineers, or trade group may not agree with what appears in the press or on the local news, but the views reflected represent those of your customers and critics.

2. **Only discuss substantial achievements.** As with eco-advertising, your credibility will be damaged if you tout

marginal improvements or non-achievements. In such cases, it is better to say nothing. The media is generally cautious about providing free advertising space—it is especially loath to being used by companies that want to build an unwarranted green image.

Topics to avoid include:

- Nonspecific *intentions* to reduce emissions or pollution.

- Changes undertaken as the result of regulations. (For example, if the law says you must eliminate a certain substance or raise underground storage tanks, then don't tout the fact that your doing so.)

- Improvement of standards to attain minimal levels for your industry.

Topics worthy of mention to the press include:

- Significant reductions in solid waste or emissions.

- Preservation of natural resources.

- The use of new technologies that recover or recycle solvents and other process materials.

- The results of new incentive programs. (Don't just announce a program, wait until you have something to show for it.)

- Awards bestowed by national environmental organizations.

- Amounts invested in pollution abatement equipment.

- Executive summaries or key points of papers and presentations given at forums, conferences, and seminars.

3. **Be specific and support your claims**. As with environmental advertising, the need for specificity and support is crucial. If you're announcing a new environmentally sound product, explain why the product causes less waste or pollution. If you or an independent source conducted tests on the product, give results. Whenever possible, offer validation from a respected third-party source.

    If your goal is to discuss the timetable for a cleanup effort, give milestone dates when various phases of the project will be complete. This information will have more of an impact if you present how it will directly affect people in the community.

4. **Avoid discussing your achievements in terms of "trees saved" and other equivalencies**. In general, the media appreciates equivalencies—they help the reading, listening, and viewing public grasp the significance of a fact or statistic. But equivalencies have been grossly overplayed in the environmental field, and talking about the number of trees saved and the like has become meaningless. Just tell it like it is, pound for pound, ton for ton, and so on.

5. **Be focused**. As in any PR effort, it's critical to identify whom you are trying to reach. A well-developed environmental PR campaign will be geared toward a clearly defined constituency. If you're trying to build relations with the local community, focus on issues of particular concern to those in the surrounding area. If you're trying to establish your company as a national or international leader, discuss how your company is dealing with large-scale environmental issues that affect the industry as a whole.

Finally, as with any kind of public relations, constant exposure leads to results. As long as you are issuing meaningful press releases, you will not incur the wrath of the editors, reporters, producers, and others who determine what makes the news and what lands in the trash can. In fact, if you are providing genuinely interesting material, they'll welcome your release—you may even enjoy positive press.

NEWSLETTERS AND OTHER COMMUNICATION VEHICLES

Newsletters

Newsletters are an excellent means for conveying your environmental accomplishments to your employees, your stakeholders, and the media. The key factor that will determine the success of your publication is commitment. An environmental publication, even one for in-house use only, should be a serious undertaking. First, if the publication dies after two issues, you'll be making an indirect statement about your environmental program—will that wither on the vine, too? To ensure that your publication continues, you have to be willing to allocate the necessary time, people, and money. Once you make a commitment, bear the following advice in mind:

1. **Designate an editor and editorial board.** Too often, newsletters and other publications are left up to administrative assistants to write and produce. When it comes to environmental publications, this can be a disastrous practice; as previously discussed, all such communications with the outside world must reflect a deep understanding of the issues, the facts, the controversies, and the potential "information land mines." Choose someone from your company who has a good sense of the

environmental field and stays abreast of current trends, articles, books, and so on.

In a large company, you might also want to appoint an ad hoc review board that represents the optimum blend of available technical and business knowledge. Members of the board should only serve if they can invest the time to seriously review articles for accuracy and breadth.

2. **Establish a realistic publication schedule.** Although it's tempting to plan for a monthly environmental publication, be aware that even publishing a four-page newsletter every month can be a major chore if you're not in the newsletter creation business. Consider starting with a quarterly publication, then increasing the schedule to six times a year or more as your proficiency improves. You're far better off beginning with a modest publication schedule and meeting your deadlines than finding yourself in a situation in which you're constantly trying to play "catch-up."

3. **Focus on informing and educating.** Just as vague advertising slogans and press releases will be greeted with skepticism, a newsletter with nonspecific topics or self-hype will be tossed before it's read. Empty generalities from your company's officers should also be avoided. In short, be positive but avoid a self-congratulatory tone. Your environmental publication's voice should be one of objective authority.

4. **Develop an editorial calendar.** Even a simple environmental newsletter requires advance planning. Plan out at least half a year's worth of feature articles; if one of your articles coincides with a current environmental event, you can always shift the calendar. Also, plan for

a variety of topics. In general, an environmental news-letter should contain one or two features and a series of short articles and "briefs." Feature articles might include topics such as:

- Environmental challenges and opportunities facing your company's industry . . . and how your company is dealing with them.

- How new environmental legislation will affect the way your company does business and the way its people do their jobs.

- The details of new pollution prevention programs at your company.

- Interviews with environmental specialists on your company's staff.

- Editorials—op-ed pieces in which people in your company air their views on pressing environmental issues and how your industry and company should respond.

Short takes and briefs might include:

- Results of pollution and waste-reduction programs.

- Educational opportunities that your company sponsors.

- Summaries of important studies relating to your industry.

- "For further reading. . . ." (books and other literature).

- Employee tips for creating "greener" work places and working in a more environmentally sound manner; ideas that employees can use at home to conserve, recycle, and curb pollution.

Finally, consider a reader's forum—a newsletter can be an excellent way to stimulate dialogue with your employees and stakeholders. You can also use the forum to identify people inside and outside the company who might contribute to feature articles in future editions.

5. **Use appropriate materials.** A slick newsletter printed on coated stock will convey the wrong message. These days, recycled paper is widely available in a variety of finishes. Show the spirit of your environmental publication by supporting the recycling economy. Better yet, have your printer use non-petroleum based inks, such as those that use soy oils as the carrier.

6. **Create a comprehensive distribution list.** Identify all of your internal and external constituents who would be interested in learning about the environmental issues related to your industry and about your company's environmental achievements. Also, be sure to develop a list of reporters and editors (including those of local and community publications); you can build name-recognition as an environmental leader through repeated exposure from your newsletter and regular press releases. And be sure that your newsletter is available to people in the surrounding community (you might also want to include a section that describes how your company is helping to better the community's environment through household hazardous waste collections and other outreach programs).

Other Publications

In addition to newsletters, you might find it worthwhile to create special environmental bulletins outlining your company's achievements. Occasional "green reports" can also be effective in summarizing key information and project results. Many of the principles previously described for newsletters also apply to this type of communication. Make sure they are written by a knowledgeable individual and that you keep the publications focused on the facts and substantive information.

COMMUNITY OUTREACH

Local Cleanup Campaigns

In addition to publicizing your environmental intentions and accomplishments, a good way to send a message to the community is through a household hazardous waste (HHW) collection program. The number of such programs has grown dramatically in a very short time. The first was conducted in 1981; more than 3,500 have been held since then. HHW collection programs range from one-time, one-day collections to regular programs conducted at multiple sites over many days to permanent, fixed facilities.

"We've seen a steady increase in business involvement in HHW collection programs, including a growing number of corporations getting involved," says Elizabeth McCormick, manager of household hazardous wastes for Laidlaw Environmental Services, the second-largest hazardous waste management company in the country and a pioneer in HHW programs. Laidlaw has handled more than 600 HHW collection programs for communities across the United States. "They're very positive programs," she continues. "What else can people do when they have hazardous materials in their garages?"

Community service groups, such as the League of Women Voters or the Rotary Club, are often the first to express an interest in a household hazardous waste collection program. Other programs have been initiated by state mandate, local businesses, or individuals who take their concerns to their city councils or county governments. Once there is a consensus that such a program is needed, it usually takes about a year before a pilot program starts. "A common cycle begins when interest is expressed, then people find out such a program is a lot of work, then interest rises again, they learn that funding is a hassle, interest grows, they begin to line up sponsors and volunteers, and the pilot is set," McCormick says.

Most HHW collection programs hit their stride when the community forms a steering committee. Local businesses that participate on the committee benefit from a perfect opportunity to do some community networking. "People who wouldn't normally speak to each other sit down and work cooperatively to pull off one of these HHW programs," McCormick says. "You've got a hazardous waste company, regulatory agency, community members, government groups, and representatives from business and industry—all focused on one issue. They can develop a good working relationship through this process."

Laidlaw recommends that communities interested in conducting an HHW collection program begin with a pilot program. "A pilot program gives a community a chance to resolve such issues as where to hold it, how to reach out to the community, and how to fund it," says McCormick. "Based on the information gathered from the pilot, a community may want to go to multiple sites, multiple collection days, or a permanent site."

The two greatest obstacles to establishing an HHW collection program are cost and liability. When people call for an estimate of the cost, McCormick offers the following suggestion: Take the number of households in the program's target area, multiply that number by 1 percent (the number likely to participate), then multiply that number by $100. "I tell people this is a guesstimate," she says. "It may be half that

123

or twice it, but at least they now have a range. With almost no federal money and limited state money available for such programs, the community must bear the cost."

The liability issues seldom stop a program from happening, but they do slow it down. The best way to address all three liability issues is to seek expert legal advice and then plan the program and any contingencies very carefully. It also helps to consider that 3,500 HHW collection programs have only produced a very limited number of small incidents. With thoughtful consideration of the cost and liability issues, a company can provide a valuable service to its community by sponsoring or participating in a local HHW collection program. And in doing so, it will communicate and support an important message about its commitment to improving the environment for everyone within the corporate sphere.

Educational Programs

Many companies offer educational materials about the environment to schools, colleges, and adult education programs. Laidlaw Environmental Services has demonstrated the extent to which a company can provide educational assistance through its Earth Academy. The Earth Academy consists of "faculty" members from Laidlaw's staff who prepare lectures and demonstrations for students in kindergarten through college. Laidlaw has also developed course material—booklets, videos, and so on—that is geared toward each age group and helps teachers integrate environmental issues into their course work. Through the Earth Academy, students learn about recycling, the causes and solutions of pollution, and how to live more environmentally responsible lives.

Although not every company is prepared for such a comprehensive educational campaign, there are always possibilities for using your technical people to convey important information about the environment. For example:

■ Sponsor an environmental teach-in at one of your sites every two months or every quarter.

■ Encourage qualified employees to teach a course as part of local adult education programs.

■ If your facility offers examples of environmental innovations, make them available to school groups for on-site visits.

■ Make your technical staff available to aid local municipalities in addressing specific environmental problems.

Remember, the goal is not simply to tout your company's environmental achievements but to teach community participants about topics such as:

■ Recycling.

■ Transportation alternatives.

■ Alternatives to environmentally harmful materials.

■ Proper use and disposal of hazardous household materials.

■ Source reduction.

Finally, consider making donations to local and national environmental causes. Hewlett Packard has won the praise of many environmentalists for its donations to the National Wildlife Fund and Nature Conservancy. Each time a toner cartridge is returned to Hewlett Packard rather than discarded,

HP donates 50 cents to each group. That keeps money flowing into the groups and toner cartridges out of landfills. HP cuts its manufacturing costs and wins support from two organizations with large memberships.

Whatever donation you make, just be sure that it's meaningful and noteworthy—otherwise, you risk being criticized for exploiting the cause that you're supporting. Also, a donation program is not enough—it must be coupled with an ongoing environmental PR campaign, a communications program, and various community outreach efforts. When you demonstrate your firm commitment on all these fronts, you'll maximize your chances of successfully promoting your message and building trust.

CHOOSING AN OUTSIDE FIRM TO HELP WITH YOUR ENVIRONMENTAL PR EFFORTS

Although it is quite possible to manage an environmental PR campaign from inside (some large companies such as AT&T have created a special PR division that works exclusively on environmental issues), you might also want to consider bringing in outside assistance. (This can be especially valuable if your company is involved with an environmental mishap and needs PR advice.) If so, here are some guidelines for choosing and working with the right PR firm:

1. **Only consider PR agencies that have proven expertise with environmental issues.** It's important that the agency thoroughly understand the particular issues facing your company, product, or service. In the case of an environmental mishap, it's critical that the firm also has expertise with crisis management.

2. **Look for a firm that will bring fresh ideas and**

knowledge to your organization. Although you will want the PR firm to work with your company's programs, you'll also want new ideas and input for environmental actions that will be well received by stakeholders and the surrounding community. Again, by working with a firm that knows the environmental field, you'll boost your chances of learning about new ideas and approaches to old problems.

3. **Provide appropriate technical information**. Don't assume that the PR firm will automatically grasp the unique message that your firm wants to convey to the world. Work closely and regularly with the firm to ensure that it's working as a partner as well as an advisor.

4. **Maintain a steady flow of information from your company to your PR firm**. Keep your PR firm apprised of your employees' solutions to environmental problems and of your company-wide success with recycling, pollution reduction, and other environmental programs. Good environmental behavior and practices might become "business as usual" in your company, but it's always fuel for a well-oiled PR machine.

5. **Define your goals as part of a long-term PR strategy**. Make sure you and your PR firm agree on the objectives of your PR program and where it will lead. Avoid a short-term approach that may leave you hanging with a conspicuous lack of a clear message that relates to pertinent environmental issues.

THE KEY TO EFFECTIVE ENVIRONMENTAL PR

1. **Convey messages worth reporting.** Good environmental PR tells a story about meaningful events that demonstrate your company's commitment to responsible practices or about ways that people in other companies can improve their environmental behavior on the job and at home.

2. **Speak constantly.** As with any public relations campaign, constant exposure is the key to success. Environmental PR is an ongoing effort that links your company to the surrounding community.

3. **Speak through many media.** Press releases, newsletters, bulletins, community outreach campaigns—the more media you use to spread worthwhile messages, the better the chances that your stakeholders and the outside world will listen.

4. **Speak promptly and completely.** If your company does suffer an environmental mishap, tell the entire story immediately, including details about how you're addressing it, what you'll do to avoid it in the future, and how you will mitigate the effect in the community. Then move on.

CHAPTER 7

STRATEGIC PARTNERSHIPS
Building Bridges over Troubled Waters

They call it "Rubbertown," eight chemical manufacturing plants along a river just west of Louisville, Kentucky. During World War II, the plants, which produced synthetic rubber, were a source of pride to the people who lived in the small towns nearby. They had little concern about emissions or toxic waste at the time—or in the fifties, sixties, and seventies, for that matter. The plants, owned by Rohm and Haas, DuPont, American Synthetic Rubber, and several other manufacturers, were simply accepted as neighbors.

All that changed during the eighties with the growing national concern about environmental dangers. Many of the once-grateful community members joined environmental activists in challenging the plants' safety records and practices; in turn, the plants' management stonewalled and dug in their heels. The battle lines were drawn for an acrimonious debate that tore at the very fabric of Rubbertown's unique sense of identity.

The tension came to a head in the mid-eighties when Rohm and Haas determined that it needed to construct a hazardous waste incinerator near one of its plants in Rubbertown. As an alternative to head-butting, the company discovered a way to serve all parties involved: the creation of a community advisory council (CAC) that would bring together people from both the factories and the surrounding area to review their relationships and find mutually acceptable solutions to problems. Today, the Rubbertown CAC has 15 members representing diverse constituencies in the area. Individuals from all eight chemical plants sit in on the CAC meetings and respond to their concerns. Although both sides must make compromises, they agree that cooperation is a vast improvement over confrontation.

Ten years ago, it was unheard of for a manufacturer (especially one in the chemical business) to form strategic partnerships with community members or long-standing adversaries such as environmental activists. Today, such partnerships are helping companies across the country improve their environmental track records and promote communication and goodwill in their communities. More companies are beginning to realize that such alliances enable them to bring broader knowledge and expertise to bear on an environmental issue or problem, to discover common ground with community members and other stakeholders, and to cultivate a more open and tolerant attitude among members of the industry and its critics.

This chapter describes potential partnerships between companies and communities and between companies and environmental organizations. It covers the benefits, steps for building a partnership, and potential pitfalls that can thwart good intentions.

FORMING COMMUNITY PARTNERSHIPS

Community relations have become a top priority for any company that has a significant environmental impact on its host communities. The preceding chapter talked about how household hazardous waste collection can be an effective way to involve your company with local environmental concerns. For companies whose presence is more strongly felt (and perhaps opposed) in their communities, a more active approach may be needed. Many have been using CACs as a vehicle for improving communication. You can learn from their experiences how to form and maintain panels and how to benefit from their input.

Community Advisory Councils

In 1985, Rohm and Haas's George Bochanski, manager of environmental communications, was sent out to the field to find a company that was able to site a hazardous waste incinerator without launching a storm of protest from the surrounding community. He found none. Every incinerator proposal was at one point thwarted by the "NIMBY (Not In My Back Yard) Syndrome."

Bochanski mused that his company might have better luck if he could persuade some of the locals to meet with plant management on a regular basis as members of a community advisory council. People from the community responded well to this surprising offer, and shortly afterwards the plant managers from two facilities chose the initial members for two CACs, one in Louisville, the other in Bristol. The members comprised a mix of local government officials, educators, homeowners, small business managers, and environmentalists. Rohm and Haas promised the two CACs that it would be open and forthright with information about the plant and would try to use the council to talk about plans for the future. In exchange, it asked the council members to use the CAC meetings as a vehicle for helping the plants' management to understand the community's concerns and needs.

At the Louisville facility, the plant manager requested that the local CAC help with the process of finalizing the proposal for the incinerator. The council reviewed Rohm and Haas's risk assessments and voiced additional areas of concern, such as how to handle the transportation of hazardous waste. "We charged them with the responsibility of making their own judgments about what would be an acceptable facility," Bochanski says. Rohm and Haas even footed the bill for a number of CAC members to visit BASF facilities in Germany, which operated incinerators similar to the one proposed for Louisville. This gave the CAC members the opportunity to talk with members of a community near an incinerator similar to the one that would be in their own area.

"The council had a significant impact on the incinerator design process," says Thomas Archibald, Louisville's plant manager. "The design of the incinerator changed because of their input." So did the plant's relationship with its community. "This wouldn't have happened without the structure of the CAC," adds Bochanski. "If we had made this proposal and a community group had come to the plant manager with its concerns, we probably would have looked at it in a more traditional sense: 'Thanks for your comments, but we'll decide.' Instead, the CAC helped shape the questions that needed to be asked."

As it turned out, the incinerator was never built, primarily because building cost estimates rose dramatically at the same time that the costs of shipping waste off-site for incineration were decreasing. But the foundation and role of the Louisville CAC had been established. "The advantage of having a specific proposal on the table is that it helped a new group develop its character and feel its way through the process," says Bochanski.

Some community members worried that the resolution of the incinerator issue would also mark the end of the CAC, but that has not happened. "We had a planning meeting after the incinerator issue was resolved and council members were interested in so many topics we still haven't finished them all," says Daniel Hicks, the Louisville plant's community relations manager. "Plus, the changeover in members means we return to major issues. We haven't seen interest waning at all."

As Rohm and Haas discovered, the makeup and focus of CACs can change as they evolve. In the case of the Louisville CAC, term limits assure an orderly flow of new faces—and new ideas—into the groups. Plant managers are encouraged to invite their most vocal critics into the CAC, which many have done. Archibald sees value in their challenges. "It's tough for us to sit here and imagine what the outside world thinks of us. The easy way is to say we know what's right, we know what we're doing and, therefore, we should keep on doing it. That's an arrogant attitude. The challenges of our council members force us to think harder about what one of our customers thinks of us." Adds Bochanski, "It's often a revelation to plant managers when the anonymous voice on the phone turns out to be a real person who is rational and interested and has legitimate concerns."

Every two years Rohm and Haas surveys the communities in which it has facilities. The surveys show steady gains in both recognition and favorability, yet Bochanski is quick to caution against attributing those gains solely to the CACs. "We stress that CACs are only one of the activities the company is pursuing in the area of communication, which is just one part of our environmental effort. CACs are an arrow in the quiver. If all you do is talk and you don't have programs designed to improve how the facility looks and smells, resolve traffic issues, or improve other community concerns, talking isn't going to get you very far."

Finally, CACs force people to be more open to and tolerant of other viewpoints through talking, listening, and striving for consensus. The spirit of cooperation makes it possible to achieve the shared goal of real environmental progress.

Forming a Community Advisory Council

1. **Identify your objectives.** The first and most critical step is to be clear internally about your goals. Rohm and Haas's Bochanski strongly recommends that you "make sure early on that there are no misunderstandings; you're better off not communicating if you're going to be selective. And you'd better plan on being in it for the long-term, because once you start this, it's very hard to stop."

2. **Gain ownership.** A community advisory council will not succeed if it has been formed by corporate edict; plant management must embrace the process. One of the best ways for getting plant management to do so is to introduce your people to other plant managers who can share their experiences with community panels. "Plant managers need to see that their peers survive the experiences, that they come out of a CAC meeting whole," says Bochanski.

3. **Establish a steering committee.** Diane Sheridan, an independent facilitator working with five community advisory committees in Texas and Kansas, advises her clients to set up steering committees, composed of community members, to help them establish their CAC panels. "I prefer to use a steering committee because a

company does a better job when it brings in community opinion leaders to assess the feasibility and desirability of a panel and to help shape the panel," she says. The steering committee addresses such issues as who will sit in on the panel, the panel's mission, and ground rules by which the panel will operate.

4. **Establish the panel.** Most people who are asked to serve on an advisory panel say "yes"; the opportunity to listen and share concerns is a welcome one. Prospective members who are skeptical of the company's motives are often reassured by a clear mission and ground rules that help them understand what the panel's role— and their role in it—will be.

   Early panel meetings focus on getting acquainted. "I like to do introductory things," Sheridan says, "including why the company wanted to form the panel, how the panel was formed, its mission and goals, and the expectations for the next few years. Between the first and second meeting I invite the panel members to talk to five to ten people in the community and ask them what they think the panel members should be saying and doing. We talk about this during the second meeting. By the third meeting I've categorized the responses and the panel begins to prioritize them. Then they choose an issue and begin to work on it."

5. **Be patient and persistent.** Like any group, an advisory panel goes through stages that some have called "forming, storming, norming, and performing." Reflective periods are followed by productive periods, which in turn are followed by reflective periods. Regular evaluations help assure the panel and company that progress toward objectives and communication goals is being made. Interest and involvement are maintained by making sure

135

panel members know they are having an impact on the company. "What keeps people on these panels is the feeling that they're doing something useful, which in this case means influencing the company and improving the quality of life in their communities," Sheridan insists.

WORKING WITH ENVIRONMENTAL ORGANIZATIONS

In addition to better community relations, companies engaged in environmental studies, audits, or assessments can greatly benefit from the expertise of outside environmental organizations. But are they willing to work with businesses, given their traditionally adversarial relationship?

Yes. The times have changed. Consider Douglas Hall's comments in the April 1992 issue of *Communication World*. Hall, who serves as the director of communication for the 600,000-member Nature Conservancy, remarked that:

Smart companies know that environmental concerns will continue to affect their work (and customer base) far into the future. Smart nonprofits need to put more trust in the longevity of their issues by demanding quality and diversity in their relationships with corporations. . . . Just as we continue to need advocacy groups to push agendas of both industry and the environment, we increasingly need groups who can act strategically as catalysts for a truer greening of business.

And Kathryn Fuller, president of the 670,000-member World Wildlife Fund, had this to say:

. . . While still not abandoning their vital role as environmental advocates, groups like World Wildlife Fund are exploring ways to work with corporations to make

136

sure that business ventures respond to environmental concerns. In part, we realize that halting economic growth is not only impractical, but also is a disservice to the millions of poor people who desperately need stronger financial underpinnings to their daily lives. But more importantly, environmental management of the planet will require a variety of solutions that are far beyond the capacity of either governments or environmental organizations to devise.

A Prototypical Partnership: McDonald's and EDF

McDonald's discovered the value of teaming up with an environmental organization in the summer of 1990 after it took a public drubbing for its use of the polystyrene clamshell in packaging. McDonald's listened to its critics, and to overcome its lack of knowledge about solid waste issues sought assistance from the Environmental Defense Fund (EDF), which had approached the company earlier with an offer to help. "We thought it might be worth proposing a dialogue to find common objectives and to work jointly on solving a problem we both wanted to solve," says Richard Denison, senior scientist at EDF.

On August 1, 1990, the fast-food giant and the outspoken environmental group formed a joint task force comprised of four McDonald's officials and three solid waste experts from EDF, led by Denison. They began their partnership by drafting a formal agreement. "The formal agreement was an excellent step because it defined what was important to each party," says Robert Langert, director of environmental affairs at McDonald's and a member of the task force. "We wanted them to get hands-on experience in our business because we wanted practical solutions."

137

Denison agrees. "The intention of the agreement was to make sure both the perceptions and the subject of the task force was oriented toward real worth and not simply window dressing." The agreement stipulated that McDonald's could not use EDF's name in its advertising and that EDF would not accept any money from McDonald's for its work on the task force. The agreement also called for the release of a public document when the work of the task force was completed and included a provision that either side could terminate its participation in the task force at any time.

Within six months, no one had thoughts of quitting, and the formal agreement had been supplanted by an open, cooperative relationship. McDonald's opened its books to the three EDF members, providing such information as amount of waste, what was being purchased, and types of materials being used. The EDF members had access to all department heads. They toured suppliers' facilities. They worked in the restaurants as fry cooks and bun flippers. All of these experiences helped them understand McDonald's business, a prerequisite to offering practical suggestions.

"They came in with a very good approach, with good, sound science," Langert says. "They weren't the radical stereotype that many people have of environmental groups. In fact, I found them to be the most logical group I've worked with."

Denison expresses a similar respect for his McDonald's colleagues. "Once they decided to do this, they were interested in doing as much as possible. In fact, the McDonald's communication officer on the task force was the first to suggest shifting the emphasis from making recommendations to implementing an action plan that the company would commit to carrying out. That change in focus gave our plan more teeth than any other plan I've seen."

The change in focus was backed by a lot of hard work.

Langert estimates that the time he and his colleagues dedicated to the task force was close to 100 percent of their work time—and that was on top of their regular jobs. He also believes it was very rewarding. "It's very rare that a big company like McDonald's can set aside that much time to go into depth about a particular aspect of running a business, in this case, solid waste. It was a rare opportunity, which is probably why we came up with rare results."

The result was a Waste Reduction Policy and a comprehensive Waste Reduction Action Plan that the task force presented in a consensus report in April 1991. The Action Plan contains 42 initiatives, pilot projects, and tests in the areas of source reduction, reuse, recycling, and composting. By the summer of 1992, McDonald's had completed 19 of the action items. It had also added 20 new initiatives.

The Action Plan led to McDonald's eliminating the clamshells; converting to unbleached paper products (for use in such items as carry-out bags); reducing the amount of paper used in napkins by reducing their size by one inch; and conducting numerous recycling, composting, and packaging tests. On a larger scale, McDonald's established an independent company called TriAce to manage solid waste and recycling within its corporate system.

Not every initiative produced positive results, however. For example, McDonald's could not find a satisfactory way to eliminate lids on cold drinks. Small children spilled the lidless cups, causing slippery floors, and it was difficult to identify diet drinks, which was especially important to diabetics. The company continues to evaluate other options, and new ideas are appearing all the time. "The report we generated with EDF has really energized people," Langert says. "I'm overwhelmed by the initiatives that have surfaced by themselves."

EDF also recognizes the benefits of its partnership with McDonald's. "We learned a great deal about how corporate

139

decision-making works," says Denison, "and that's helped us hone our skills in terms of putting ideas we believe are important into a context that addresses and reflects practical business considerations. We learned about the clout McDonald's has, as a large customer, to influence the environmental practices of its suppliers. And we came to appreciate how change occurs in a corporation. It has to be incremental. There isn't any grand slam here, just a lot of singles. We devised a way to look systematically at all McDonald's does and move ahead on a number of fronts at once."

For its part, McDonald's has thoroughly assessed its environmental management system, identified areas for improvement, and initiated action. In less than two years it has gone from environmental neophyte to environmental leader. That was the power of its strategic partnership.

EDF continues to pursue strategic partnerships, and in 1992 it announced a pending agreement with General Motors. The EDF/GM partnership is more open-ended than the partnership with McDonald's and has the potential to address a broader range of issues.

HOW TO FORM A PARTNERSHIP WITH AN ENVIRONMENTAL GROUP

1. **Identify environmental issues your company needs to address.** The process begins with an assessment of your company's environmental standing and a list of objectives. With this in hand, you can look for areas where input from an environmental group can help your company achieve its goals. Remember, the purpose of a partnership with an environmental group is to address environmental issues, not just to share opinions or de-

bate options. Before agreeing to join a partnership, both sides must recognize the opportunity for it to produce something of value.

2. **Contact environmental groups.** There are roughly 30 major environmental organizations worldwide (see the Appendix). In the United States, the largest environmental groups include:

- The National Wildlife Federation (more than 6 million members and an annual budget approaching $100 million).

- World Wildlife Fund (670,000 members).

- The Nature Conservancy (600,000 members).

- The National Audubon Society (550,000 members).

- Sierra Club (500,000 members; $32 million budget).

- Wilderness Society (300,000 members).

- Natural Resources Defense Council (125,000 members).

- Environmental Defense Fund (100,000 members; $15 million budget).

Most of these groups have local chapters and are experienced at discussing environmental issues with businesses. Ask each group you contact about its particular areas of expertise and interests. Remember, environmental organizations are constantly barraged with requests for endorsements and partnerships. Make sure your appeal makes sense in terms of its subject, scope, and focus.

3. **Establish a formal, working arrangement.** A formal agreement reassures both sides that neither will be taken advantage of by its new ally. The agreement should define the purpose and objectives of the partnership, the roles each side will play in it, the issues that will be addressed, a rough timeline indicating when key steps will occur, and an escape clause that allows either side to end the partnership at any time.

4. **Commit to achieving the partnership's objectives.** McDonald's gained the greatest value from its partnership with EDF because it opened itself up for scrutiny by EDF's task force members, it invested four people's time in the study of a specific environmental issue, and it initiated improvements based on the task force's recommendations.

   Although maintaining such a partnership is very hard work, it only marks the beginning of a long-term, ongoing effort that a company must make to improve its environmental quality management. The value of such a strategic partnership is to jump-start the improvement process; it is the company's responsibility to make sure the process keeps going. As the Nature Conservancy's Douglas Hall remarked, "We look for signs of commitment beyond the initial handshake. The daily barrage of calls we get suggesting product endorsements, special events, and member list sales has forced us to think strategically about the nature and duration of our corporate couplings. Call us old fashioned, but we wisely favor long-term, multifaceted relationships."

OTHER OPPORTUNITIES FOR PARTNERSHIPS

In addition to working with community and environmental organizations, companies today have a broad range of opportunities for working with other businesses—even competitors—as well as local, state, and federal government. Several such options are described in the following sections.

Utilities

Utility companies are often on the leading edge of efforts to improve energy efficiency and promote conservation. Many have established technology or energy centers that disseminate information about energy-efficient technologies and their economic benefits and work with companies to help them improve in this area. "One of the major barriers to implementing energy efficiency programs is a lack of information on business's part," says Claude Poncelet, manager of corporate environmental initiative for Pacific Gas and Electric. "When we show that energy bills can be significantly reduced by investing in more efficient equipment—and that we are here to help [companies] do that—[they] are very receptive." All that is required to make your local utility into an ally is awareness of the need to improve energy efficiency and a phone call.

Government Agencies

Many companies work with state and regional agencies to solicit ideas and advice and to form task forces, committees, advisory panels, and other types of partnerships focused on specific issues. The first step in working with a government agency is to see it as an ally and not an adversary. As Conoco

143

CEO Constantine Nicandros says, "We need government, the environmental community, and other concerned citizens as partners sensitive to the competitive global challenges we face. Without these partners, internal efforts keeping operations lean and efficient will simply not be enough to provide us the means to remain a major competitive force in a global economy."

Local Businesses

Local business enterprises share a desire to improve environmental quality in their communities. The increased interest in environmental issues has prompted more communication, information sharing, and joint studies by the environmental, health, and safety directors of companies with similar agendas. In a growing number of municipalities, this cooperation has been formalized as companies create partnerships to address the environmental concerns of their communities. The most common participants are chemical companies, oil refiners, and paper mills, although companies with similar environmental problems and goals may join forces regardless of the nature of their businesses.

Trade Associations

Chemical manufacturers have long been targeted as adversaries by environmental activists. In 1985, the Canadian Chemical Producers introduced a program called Responsible Care with the goal of establishing environmental standards for the chemical industry while encouraging a cooperative spirit to achieve them. The Chemical Manufacturers Association (CMA) in the United States adopted the program in 1988.

The foundation of Responsible Care is a set of standards,

144

the Codes of Management Practice, which covers every aspect of a chemical company's environmental management program, including emergency response, pollution prevention, and employee health and safety. CMA members must conduct annual self-evaluations of where they are in relation to each of the codes. The CMA developed the codes with input from a public advisory panel it formed for this purpose. The panel, which consists of 15 people representing a diversity of backgrounds, constituencies, and geographic areas, meets five or six times a year to evaluate and suggest improvements in the proposed codes. Although panel members still see weaknesses in the process, most notably the absence of external audits, they recognize that Responsible Care is not just another public relations ploy.

"Everybody on the panel started with suspicions," says Don Lesh, a panel member representing the Global Tomorrow Coalition. "We've concluded that, while it's not a perfect process, the CMA hasn't been pursuing this for cosmetic reasons. I've been most impressed with the fact that, once the codes are in place, a company's acceptance of them is the criteria for acceptance in the CMA."

"The CMA has 175 members who produce over 90 percent of the industrial petrochemicals manufactured in the U.S.," says John Holtzman, CMA's vice-president of communications, "and all of them are part of Responsible Care. The remaining 10 percent is produced by small companies who don't want to or can't afford to participate in CMA. We created Responsible Care partnerships that allow them to take advantage of the program without joining CMA."

The codes are also being studied by companies in other industries. For example, the codes written for community awareness and emergency response (CAER) could be used by organizations made up of steel, electronics, or other types of companies.

If your industry has struggled with environmental issues, chances are it has a trade association addressing them. Trade associations help companies with legal, technical, and regulatory issues; provide a forum for the transfer of environmental information; pool resources to conduct environmental studies; and unite like-minded companies in achieving shared environmental goals.

Organizations or associations that bring companies with similar objections together provide an excellent forum for addressing common environmental issues. Larger companies are also forming partnerships with leaders from other industries to focus attention on shared environmental concerns.

PITFALLS OF BUILDING STRATEGIC PARTNERSHIPS

As beneficial as strategic partnerships may prove to be, your company and its partner must overcome numerous hurdles that can slow progress or even destroy the relationship. Whatever type of partnership your company is considering or is already involved in, keep the following pitfalls in mind:

1. **Lack of Commitment.** If a company is not willing to participate fully in the partnership, the sharing of information and expertise will have very little effect on the company's environmental management. That includes following through on concerns and actions requested by the partners. The members of the environmental group or CAC must also demonstrate commitment to making the partnership work. Ellie Skokan, undergraduate coordinator for Wichita State University's Department of Biological Sciences, has been a member of a community advisory panel since its formation in 1988. "It takes a lot of time and energy to be an effective panel member," she says. "A lot of people aren't able or willing to give

that much, which means their contributions aren't effective."

2. **Lack of Trust.** In speaking of his involvement on the CMA's Public Advisory Panel, environmentalist Don Lesh expressed concern about what role he and other panel members were playing. "We don't want to be part of a corporate greenwashing." The fear of being compromised or co-opted is common on the noncompany side of a partnership. And that fear does not go away easily. Skokan says: "As the company does more outreach in the community, I'm concerned that people on the advisory panel are also from the institutions benefitting from the company's outreach. It's something you have to be aware of." From the company's viewpoint, the openness required by a partnership exposes the company to harsh criticism and adverse publicity. The best immediate solution is a written agreement that spells out what each side can and cannot do. The best long-term solution is the evolution of mutual respect between allies working together toward common goals.

3. **Lack of Planning.** If partnerships lack a clear plan, they tend to meander from issue to issue, reacting to a member's latest complaint or spending too much time talking and not enough time acting. The slightest glitch can become an overwhelming obstacle. By contrast, good partnerships begin with mutual agreement about the partners' goals and objectives. The McDonald's/EDF partnership provides an excellent example of how effective planning can make a partnership yield the desired results.

4. **Lack of Communication.** When communication breaks down, a partnership becomes less effective. And

with all the communication that is required to make a partnership work, breakdowns can be frequent. "People don't necessarily have good communication links," says Daniel Hicks, community relations manager for Rohm and Haas' Louisville plant. "Neighborhood representatives are a good example; there's no reporting mechanism in place. There's no way we can make sure two-way communication is as good as it should be." Mechanisms that enable a company to communicate internally what the partnership is doing may also be missing. Companies participating in strategic partnerships should therefore ensure that regular, frequent, and accurate communication takes place.

For example, Kodak spreads the word about its environmental activities by means of a special section in its annual report; by the EnvironMinute, a series of 60-second radio public service announcements; by reports on specific issues; by a report on Kodak's environmental health and safety policy; and by plant newsletters that include articles about environmental programs.

Dow Chemical's communication program focuses heavily on preparing employees to talk about environmental issues and the media to understand and interpret what it is hearing. The program includes:

- A 24-hour, toll-free media hotline for environmental issues.

- Classes to help journalists understand environmental issues.

- Media seminars on environmental issues.

- Support for Dow managers who will be giving speeches on environmental issues.

- Training for Dow scientists who will be appearing on talk shows.

- Kits for customers and plant managers with information about environmental communication.

- A newsletter distributed worldwide.

- Annual environmental reports published at various Dow locations.

When both sides bring commitment, trust, planning, and a willingness to communicate to the table, they maximize the chances of a strategic partnership achieving its most important objectives: creating the opportunity for the partners to address environmental issues more completely than either could have done alone and solving pressing environmental problems.

MAKING STRATEGIC PARTNERSHIPS WORK

1. Adopt a win-win attitude. Strategic partnerships are more than a means of placating your neighbors or gaining an endorsement; they represent an important means for all parties to achieve their goals.

2. Do your homework and choose the right partners— otherwise you may set the clock back and return to the days of adversarial relationships.

3. Know your goals. Regardless of what type of organization you wish to align yourself with, the process of choosing a partner begins with an understanding of the specific environmental need your company wishes to address and the objectives it wants to achieve.

4. To ensure the maximum benefits from a strategic partnership, draft a formal agreement and support it with commitment, trust, planning, and communication.

CHAPTER 8

VANGUARD
ENVIRONMENTAL
COMPANIES
Taking Proactive Environmental Action

Those who keep tabs on endangered species have recently added a new one to the list: unlimited growth. In its place, a fledgling concept called "sustainable development" is emerging, spawned by the need to promote environmental responsibility: "In the future, access to international markets will depend on who has the most environmentally sound technologies." So said Tsukasa Sakai, senior managing director of JGC Corporation, in the 11 May 1992 issue of *BusinessWeek*. During the 1970s and 1980s, Japanese companies continuously improved their manufacturing processes to the degree that they now use half of the materials and energy used by U.S. companies to produce one unit of GNP. Such efficiency means their products enjoy about a 5 percent cost advantage over U.S.-made products, and they are looking to build on that advantage through proactive environmental action.

In 1990, Japan announced a 100-year plan for sustainable development. For American business leaders whose imaginations are stretched by 5-year plans, a 100-year plan must seem pointless—until we consider Japan's dramatic and steady quality improvements over the past 45 years.

This chapter describes how companies can take a long-term view and act rather than react—that is, change their policies and practices before being forced to do so. We'll present examples of successful proactive environmental action at companies with some of the best track records in the business.

CHOOSE TODAY OR BE REGULATED TOMORROW

Sustainable development is rapidly replacing unlimited growth as the primary goal of companies worldwide. It means meeting our needs without compromising the ability of future generations to meet theirs and working toward a balance of economic growth and environmental protection, a balance of human activity with nature's ability to renew itself.

The idea of sustainable development has quickly gained broad appeal. The International Chamber of Commerce developed 16 principles for environmental management called the Business Charter for Sustainable Development. Companies such as Xerox have signed the charter and adopted the principles because it fits with their own sustainable development vision.

In a report on development and the environment, the Business Council for Sustainable Development, which consists of the leaders of 50 major international corporations, made these statements:

Business will play a vital role in the future health of this

152

planet. As business leaders, we are committed to sustainable development, to meeting the needs of the present without compromising the welfare of future generations.

This concept recognizes that economic growth and environmental protection are inextricably linked, and that the quality of present and future life rests on meeting basic human needs without destroying the environment on which all life depends.

Or as Gus Speth, president of World Resources Institute, described the connection between economic growth and environmental protection: "No business enterprise can be economically sound for long unless it's also ecologically sound."

Today, businesses face the choice of pursuing environmental soundness proactively as a corporate policy or to wait for regulations, customers, and employees to drag the company toward responsible policies and practices. To date, unfortunately, most are waiting to have their future handed to them on a plate.

Resisting change for as long as possible buys time, but the environment picks up the tab. In a speech to the Edison Electric Institute Energy and Environment Committee, the Sierra Club's Carl Pope remembered a representative of a major U.S. utility telling him in 1982 that "we [utility companies] understand we are going to have to clean up these emissions. We recognize that sooner or later the American people are going to demand it, but from our point of view, we want to delay that because it frees up capital for however long we can delay."

They delayed until 1990. Pope concluded, "I would argue that, as a direct consequence of this success in achieving delay, the bill which passed had both more ambitious clean-up objectives and a more compressed timetable than could have been negotiated in 1982."

By choosing to be dragged toward environmental responsibility, utility companies must now meet more stringent standards in less time than if they had negotiated an agreement in 1982. Worse yet, the delay added an estimated 50 million tons of sulfur oxides to the air that must also be cleaned up—all for the short-term, bottom-line desire to "free up capital," which may have been a poor financial decision, because more and more companies are discovering that proactive environmental action can actually be profitable.

Consider the case of Pacific Gas & Electric, which provides gas and electricity to 11 million customers across 94,000 square miles. It is one of California's top ten landowners, with more than 150 endangered and threatened species in the areas it works.

PG&E has invested more than $1.5 billion in energy conservation since the mid-1970s. The company now gets about half of its energy in an average water year from renewable technologies such as hydropower, geothermal, biomass, wind, and solar.

As a result of its conservation efforts, PG&E has saved its customers more than $3 billion. In the first six months of 1990 alone, PG&E's conservation programs earned more than $15 million for its shareholders' bottom line. The company expects demand to grow by 3300 megawatts by the year 2000. It will meet 75 percent of that demand through customer energy-efficiency and conservation measures that are already in place. That represents the equivalent of two to five major generating plants, which are about three times more expensive than implementing the conservation measures.

As PG&E's Alison Silverstein, a senior analyst, says: "This isn't something we're doing just because our customers think of themselves as environmentalists. This is something we're doing because we're going to make money at it, and it's going to be our source of competitive advantage."

GAINING A COMPETITIVE EDGE THROUGH PREEMPTIVE ENVIRONMENTAL ACTION

Businesses in a variety of industries are proving that proactive environmental action provides a competitive advantage.

For example, 3M projects that achieving its goal of reducing air and water emissions by 90 percent and solid waste by 50 percent from 1990 levels will cut the inflation-adjusted cost of most products by 10 percent. The Gillette Company uses 625 million gallons of water *less* than it used in 1972—in just one of its facilities. That alone cuts Gillette's water bill by $3 million per year. And Dow Chemical has cut its airborne pollutants in half since 1984 and plans to halve them again by 1995. The company expects to save millions by avoiding disposal and regulatory costs.

3M's ambitious goals build on the environmental management program mentioned in Chapter 1, Pollution Prevention Pays, or "3P," which it introduced in 1975.

"When we looked at all the regulations that were coming in at that time, we knew we couldn't respond from the end of the pipe, with a pollution control approach," says Tom Zosel, manager of 3M's pollution prevention programs. "We had to design out the environmental problems. Consequently, we had to build a pollution prevention ethic into the corporation."

The idea of preventing pollution and therefore minimizing the need to control it can be called a proactive—and in some cases, preemptive—strategy. For senior management to choose such a strategy, it must be convinced that the benefits will outweigh the costs. 3M has proven that they do, but that proof did not exist in the mid-1970s.

"Management really faces two choices," Zosel says. "You can spend all this for pollution control or you can ask people to design in pollution prevention. Selling prevention has been

155

easier at 3M because our last three CEO's have been chemical engineers, so they understand technical issues. And 3M is based on innovation and change, so asking people to innovate and change is a normal message. It was just a matter of sending that message in the environmental area."

The 3P program encourages technical innovation to prevent pollution at the source through:

- **Product reformulation**—developing nonpolluting or less-polluting products and processes.

- **Process modification**—changing manufacturing processes to minimize waste or incorporate nonpolluting or less-polluting materials.

- **Equipment redesign**—modifying equipment to perform better or use available resources.

- **Resource recovery**—recycling byproducts for sale or for use in other 3M products or processes.

3M anticipated four measurable benefits of its 3P program—a better environment, conserved resources, improved technologies, and reduced costs—and structured a formal recognition program based on them. To be recognized with a 3P award, a project must eliminate or reduce a pollutant that is or could be a 3M problem; reduce energy consumption, use raw materials more efficiently, or improve the use of other natural resources; involve a technical accomplishment, innovative approach, or unique design; and benefit 3M financially.

Through March 1992, 3,450 Pollution Prevention Pays projects had been recognized throughout the company, 985 of them in the United States. 3M's total worldwide savings realized through the 3P program, from 1975–1991, was *$573 million*. That's *first-year* savings. To get a real cost savings for the life of a 3P project, you can multiply this figure by 2.5. The result is a savings of more than $1.4 billion worldwide, nearly $1.2 billion in the United States. And these figures do not consider the financial and competitive benefits obtained by reducing raw materials and production costs.

Benefits to the environment have been equally impressive. By 1987, 3M had cut its pollution and energy consumption in half. By 1992, the 3P program had prevented pollution in the United States in the following areas (first-year only cumulative results):

Air pollutants	140,000 tons
Water pollutants	16,300 tons
Wastewater	1 billion gallons
Sludge/solid waste	416,000 tons

In addition, 3M's Air Emission Reduction Program has reduced air emissions by 52,000 tons annually. The company's Commute-A-Van program has saved more than 3 million gallons of gasoline and eliminated more than 60 million pounds of air emissions. And its Resource Recovery programs have recovered more than 100 million pounds of metals, plastics, solvents, papers, and other materials for reuse or sale.

"Our goal is to become a sustainable growth company," says Zosel, "because 3M believes that's what is necessary to be competitive in the next century. If you don't reduce waste, you won't be able to compete."

3M is well-positioned to compete because it acted proactively through its 3P program and other environmental initiatives. It delivers proof that doing so can be profitable and that prevention pays. As the company states, "at 3M, environmental and business goals have merged, creating a top priority for elimination of waste."

This integration of environmental and business management has made 3M a national role model. The company has provided detailed descriptions of its 3P program to more than 200 companies, and its environmental experts speak to more than 100 conferences and business groups each year. 3M has worked with congressional committees and U.S. EPA staff to promote pollution prevention, and its 3P program has become a common subject of television and newspaper reports on environmental issues. All of these efforts help promote 3M's image as a socially responsible, innovative, proactive company, an image that boosts employee morale and appeals to existing and potential customers.

3M touts its 3P program through a newsletter called *Ideas: A Compendium of 3P Success Stories.* Each page describes a 3P project, including the problem, solution, payoff, and members of the team formed to address the problem. Here are some examples from the publication:

- 3M's Cordova, Illinois, plant makes adhesives, resins, and polymers in dozens of 4,000–8,000 gallon reactors. Each reactor has to be cleaned when changing from one product to another, a task that used to require filling it with caustics or solvent and boiling the solution for one or two days. The "Doozy Kings," a quality circle at the plant, developed an alternative that included a sonic cleaning system and two-phase cleanup that involves applying chemicals under pressure. First-year savings in materials, labor, and machine costs totaled $575,000. The solution cost $36,000. It also eliminated 1,000 tons a year of water pollutants and reduced energy and disposal costs.

- Riker Laboratories, 3M's pharmaceutical plant in Northbridge, California, used to use a solvent-based process that created emission problems. Riker then developed a water-based process instead. The changes cost $60,000, but they eliminated the need to buy $180,000 in pollution control equipment, saved $15,000 a year in solvent purchases, prevented 24 tons of air pollution annually, reduced cleanup time, and improved worker comfort by eliminating unpleasant fumes.

■ A 3M plant in White City, Oregon, makes a dry silver reader printer paper used for transferring information from microfilm to paper. Drying is a critical part of the production process. Temperature control had become a problem every time the process started, causing tons of paper to be discarded. The Idea Team solved the problem by developing a highly innovative computer application to control start-up temperature, a solution that cost $16,000 but saved $533,200 annually by eliminating start-up waste products, prevented 53 tons of air pollution, and eliminated 137 tons of solid waste. And the temperature control computer technology is being adapted to other 3M facilities where precise heat control is critical.

These and other 3P ideas produce the benefits 3M seeks: a better environment, conserved resources, improved technologies, and reduced costs. They prove that proactive environmental action pays and that source reduction eliminates pollution and saves money. Although it may take several years to make environmental management a normal part of doing business, it only takes a firm corporate commitment to eliminating pollution to begin the process.

"When you look at a program that's existed for 17 years, you can see that a lot of things have changed in how we run it," Zosel says. "But the basic concept and goals have remained constant, which is why the program is still alive and well."

And the program is moving forward—3M has set ambitious goals for the next ten years, including ending the use of ozone-depleting chemicals by 1993, reducing the generation of waste by 35 percent by 1995, and reducing all environmental releases to all media by 90 percent by the year 2000. 3M's stated goal for the future is "zero releases and sustainable development."

THE NEW CORPORATE CONSERVATION ETHIC

The elimination of waste, whether that waste is pollution, unnecessary manufacturing steps, or people's time, has become a primary goal for business leaders around the world. They know that waste slows productivity and degrades quality, and they have marshalled their forces to identify and eliminate it. In environmental circles, this is called *conservation*, a philosophy many have been following for decades.

The Gillette Company is a good example of how the conservation ethic can yield results. In 1972, Gillette's economic review committee studied world issues to identify which ones would affect the company long-term. Two nonproduct issues that surfaced were energy and water. The company decided that water was a critical resource that needed to be conserved—even though the cost of water at the time was not a major consideration. So it established a water conservation policy and assigned responsibilities for conservation, preservation, and the development of alternate resources. Nothing was said about saving money.

Gillette then audited its plants, looking at consumption. It also developed a manual outlining water and energy issues, how those issues affected the company, and the company's water and energy conservation policies. The consumer product maker also set a goal to reduce its water usage by 10 percent in each plant annually.

"We have a three-part program," says Cameron Beers, Gillette's director of administrative services. "We started with *awareness*, making sure everyone from the chairman down was aware of water and energy issues and how they related to Gillette. We defined responsibilities. And we encouraged everyone to participate."

The encouragement took several forms. Gillette offered water-saving devices at cost to employees for their use at home. It also developed poster and slogan contests to keep people thinking about conservation and inserted water conservation booklets in paycheck envelopes. In addition, the company offered incentives to any employee who suggested a successful conservation measure, a bonus equal to 15 to 20 percent of the money saved during the first year of operation. While 3M's 3P program focused on technical solutions and innovation, Gillette's involved every employee in water conservation through "people power."

"Our whole philosophy has been that you get more done by cooperation and people power than by confrontation and regulation," says Beers. "Once you get people involved, the achievements always exceed your expectations."

The second part of Gillette's water conservation program is cross-fertilization, taking successful ideas from one plant and introducing them to the cross-functional conservation committees at its other plants. The committees work with the ideas to make them fit their plants' needs, often expanding and improving them in the process. This process is still a vital part of the company's conservation efforts, more than 20 years after the conservation program began.

The final element in the program is team tasks. "We use these teams for experimenting with conservation alternatives," says Beers. "For example, one team might look at solar energy, another at computer controls, and so on. Their conclusions are communicated to other plants so they don't have to reinvent the wheel. We also have regional meetings for teams to report what they're doing and share their successes."

Awareness, cross-fertilization, and team tasks, energized by "people power," have made Gillette's water conservation program an international model. Gillette's successes helped convince Massachusetts's state officials and the directors of the Massachusetts Water Resources Authority (MWRA) that efficient water use (Demand Management) should be the first step toward ensuring adequate water supplies. In turn, this MWRA program has become a model for other water utilities in the United States.

Gillette has worked with the state of California and the cities of Phoenix and Boston to assess and improve their conservation efforts. Also, companies such as Polaroid and countries such as England and Argentina have used Gillette's "people power" approach. Additionally, Gillette has helped the Universities of Virginia and Massachusetts and Harvard University develop environmental education programs.

Jane Ploeser manages Phoenix's water conservation program, one of the largest in the country. In her recommendation of Gillette for recognition by The National Environmental Awards Council and Renew America's Searching for Success program, she wrote:

> I commend Gillette for not only being the nation's first industry to institute an aggressive conservation program, but in being generous with their time and expertise with others. Private institutions who instigate such programs on their own, without government edict or environmental legislation, who do things just because they're the right thing to do, should be recognized.

Her comments capture the essence of proactive environmental action: *doing the right thing without being told to do it.* The results of such action, initiated 20 years ago, are still being tallied and enjoyed.

"The benefits of our conservation efforts are immense,"

162

Beers says. "Our employees can be proud of our achievements: we defined a critical world resource; we acted; and we're the only industry to participate with the International Energy Agency in developing a world energy policy. We've received many awards from local, state, and government agencies. When people ask what to do about water conservation, people say, 'Call Gillette.' Being a consumer company, such positive publicity certainly doesn't hurt us."

Another significant benefit is the water Gillette has conserved. In the company's South Boston plant alone, Gillette is using 625 million gallons less per year than it did in 1972, having reduced consumption from 730 million gallons to 105 million gallons. The amount of water saved is about as much as the entire Massachusetts Water Resource Authority uses over the course of two and a half days.

Finally, there's the fact that the program does save Gillette money. Water bills that were insignificant in 1972 have become major expenses in the 1990s. Gillette's financial incentive for conserving water is $3 million of savings in its South Boston plant, which is one of 57 facilities in 28 countries. It turns out that Gillette's doing the right thing for the environment led to financial rewards as well.

At 3M, pollution prevention pays. At Gillette, conservation pays. Since the 1970s, these companies have realized the payoff of proactive environmental management:

■ A better environment

■ Reduced waste

■ An enhanced corporate image

■ Employee involvement and pride

■ Conserved resources

■ Reduced costs

163

TAKING THE INITIATIVE IN ENVIRONMENTAL PROBLEM AREAS

It is always helpful when a company's cause has widespread public support. No one is against preventing pollution or conserving resources. Some may balk at the cost in time and money, but nobody quibbles with the goals. Such universal acceptance makes it easier to gain management's commitment, motivate employees, and invest in preemptive action.

Not every cause enjoys widespread support, however. McDonald's has made rapid progress in reducing waste, but it is still being criticized for not doing enough. Although several major oil companies are working aggressively on environmental management, they still suffer from a poor public image. Chemical companies that are diligently seeking alternatives to hazardous substances are still being vilified for the products they sell.

When dealing with technically complex environmental issues, even the best intentions can result in sharp criticism. Procter & Gamble learned this when it offered composting as part of the solution to the municipal solid waste problem, caused in part by disposable diapers.

Compost is a humuslike material formed when microorganisms and water are used to break down organic matter. Compost can be used to enrich topsoil, reducing the amount of chemical fertilizers needed. Most people are familiar with the compost created by leaves, grass, and food waste. It is hard to picture throwing disposable diapers into that mix and coming up with something useful—which is why you can't do it at home or as part of a municipal yard/leaf waste program.

Procter & Gamble's diapers are about 80 percent compostable; the plastic outer cover is not, although the company is developing a compostable substitute for it. The noncompostable cover means that disposable diapers can only be composted in facilities that treat an entire municipal waste stream.

As of this writing, only 22 cities or counties in 12 states have municipal solid waste composters, although P&G claims that 150 facilities in 30 states are under development. Still, much of the nation does not have access to the composting facilities necessary to keep disposable diapers out of landfills.

Even so, after identifying what they believed was the best possible solution for their company and their customers, P&G set out to promote solid waste composting. The company established a $20 million fund to advance an infrastructure for solid waste composting worldwide. The money pays for such projects as community grants to help officials learn how composting fits their solid waste management plans, education on the benefits of solid waste composting, market development to ensure outlets for the compost, scientific research into composting, and the formation of Solid Waste Composting Councils, which are organizations in the United States, Europe, Canada, and Australia working to support composting. Procter & Gamble sponsored scientific and technical seminars in the United States and Europe and helped plan an International Composting Research Symposium in 1992. All this and more has been done to accelerate the support for and development of solid waste composting facilities.

But unlike pollution prevention and water conservation, solid waste composting has its detractors. The strongest objection concerns the problems commonly encountered with composting the whole mixed waste stream. The cleaner the material to be composted, the better quality the resulting compost will be. In Europe, which has had municipal solid waste composting for decades, the trend is to separate food and yard waste at the source for composting and to avoid composting anything else because the pollutants commonly found in municipal waste, such as toxic metals from batteries and shards of plastic and glass, contaminate the end product. Compost in which the plastic outer covers of disposable diapers have not been separated would be considered "dirty" and would only be suitable for nonagricultural applications, such as landfill cover.

Procter & Gamble's preemptive strategy could have taken these concerns into consideration. It chose not to. In fact, P&G's strategy exposed the company to harsh criticism for deceptive advertising, although the company is quick to point out that the purpose of its advertising was to educate the public on the need to promote solid waste composting.

- In 1990, P&G distributed pamphlets, complete with diaper discount coupons, to more than 14 million American households describing how Luvs and Pampers can be composted. At that time, only a handful of communities had solid waste composting facilities.

- In Rhode Island, free samples of Luvs were placed on doorsteps with the message: "This product is compostable in municipal composting units. Support recycling and composting in your community." Rhode Island has no such composting facilities anywhere in the state.

- Early in 1991, P&G sponsored advertisements in a dozen major magazines showing dark brown earth under the headline, "Ninety days ago this was a disposable diaper." The ads stated that 80 percent of each diaper can be converted into a "rich, high-quality soil enhancer that's good for planting baby flowers, trees, and just about anything else that grows." The ad implies that all disposables that are composted would be suitable for agricultural applications, a claim that some environmentalists and agricultural interests questioned. Others challenged the ads for saying Luvs and Pampers are easily compostable even though few consumers have access to municipal composting facilities.

The dispute over P&G's advertising may be forgotten in the near future as more and more communities build solid waste composters, regulations are enacted to assure clean compost, and new uses for all kinds of compost are developed. The company's efforts to advance composting continue; in 1992 it cosponored a test project with the National Audubon Society in Connecticut to explore the potential for source-separated municipal composting. In time, Procter & Gamble may even be hailed as a pioneer in solid waste composting. Nevertheless, the company could have garnered more public support and less criticism had it taken into account opposing technological views and skepticism about environmental advertising.

WHERE TO TAKE PREEMPTIVE
ENVIRONMENTAL ACTION

1. **Solid waste reduction and disposal.** McDonald's efforts to reduce waste have earned praise from environmental organizations, recognition by consumers, and increased profits for the company. To learn more about the preemptive path McDonald's followed, refer to Chapter 7. The path includes an initial assessment of your solid waste situation, identification of opportunities to reduce or eliminate waste, prioritizing actions, and implementing them.

   Many corporations are getting involved in helping their communities dispose of household hazardous waste (see Chapter 6). Contact your local EPA office to find out if such opportunities exist in your community.

2. **Energy and water conservation and recycling.** Preemptive action is easier in this area than any other because most people are familiar with conservation and

recycling. Employees who recycle at home find it easy to recycle at work. People who routinely turn lights off and fix leaky faucets at home know to look for these things at work. Like solid waste reduction, a comprehensive conservation and recycling plan begins with an assessment of the situation before developing a strategy to improve it.

Your company may also wish to explore local, state, or national recycling and conservation opportunities. The Recycle Centers supported by Gillette and others provide an outlet for materials you may otherwise discard. Programs such as Green Lights, sponsored by the EPA to support the use of energy-efficient lighting, invite companies to participate in a national energy conservation initiative.

3. **Pollution prevention.** As 3M has shown, preventing pollution is good for both the environment and the company. Preemptive action begins with identifying sources of pollution and then seeking ways to prevent pollution through product reformulation, process modification, equipment redesign, or resource recovery.

4. **Packaging.** Procter & Gamble has been a leader in environmental packaging; its concentrated laundry detergents reduce packaging and costs. It is using recycled plastic in its liquid detergent bottles and has eliminated outside cartons for its deodorants, saving 3.4 million pounds of solid waste each year.

Preemptive actions in this area include:

- Considering all types of packaging, including inbound and nonproduct materials and parts packaging.

- Establishing quantitative measures of packaging waste.

168

- Reducing or eliminating packaging volume and waste.

- Using recycled plastics/paper.

5. **Standards and regulations.** Gillette, 3M, and Procter & Gamble all have a reputation for proacting on environmental issues that has enabled them to contribute to national and international environmental studies and to participate in debates at the highest levels. To act preemptively, begin by choosing an issue that is relevant to your company. Study it carefully. Involve company representatives in conferences and seminars where the issue is discussed. Explore facets of the issue within your company and in partnership with others. Share what you learn and ask to participate in discussions of local, state, national, and international standards and regulations.

STAYING AHEAD OF REGULATORS AND CRITICS

Although not every company has the luxury of choosing which environmental issues to act on, certain issues *can* be addressed in a preemptive manner by most companies. By policing yourself, you'll preempt regulators and critics. (Recall how Johnson & Johnson voluntarily instituted its protective wrapping system following the tragic Tylenol poisonings; not only did J&J win public approval for the action, but it was also able to develop a security system that met its own specifications rather than having the government hand one to it that may have been more expensive to implement.)

In the environmental arena, nothing better illustrates preemptive environmental action than Hewlett-Packard and Canon's laser toner cartridge recycling program. As described in Chapter 4, both companies make it possible to return spent cartridges rather than toss them into the local dump. The cartridges are cannibalized and used in the manufacture of new cartridges. The two companies then make donations to two major environmental organizations.

Neither company had explicitly planned the reclamation program as an effort to ward off criticism of the wastefulness of their products, but the effect is certainly a preemptive one; laser toner cartridges are a solid waste nightmare and would have likely been targeted by environmental organizations. Moreover, state or federal regulations might have mandated options far less favorable to the companies. By doing right and offering a solution to the problem, HP and Canon emerged as corporate environmental heroes. They also enjoy reduced manufacturing costs because of the materials they receive through the reclamation program. As their cases demonstrate, preemptive action often leads to win-win situations.

PROACTIVE ENVIRONMENTAL STRATEGIES

1. Take the high road to environmental issues. If you think in terms of doing right today, you'll probably do well tomorrow.

2. Train everyone in your company to think proactively; conduct "what-if" sessions in which you imagine your company under fire from activist organizations or lawmakers to improve the environmental soundness of your products and services. Then take action.

3. Look for strategic opportunities to preempt criticism from activists and lawmakers; consider all your products, processes, and services as candidates for preemptive action.

CHAPTER 9

THE NEW ENVIRONMENTAL WATCHDOGS

Gaining a Nod of Approval from the Socially Consious Investment Community

"When analysts from the traditional investment community knock at the door of major companies, they're greeted with open arms. Why shouldn't environmental auditors be treated the same way?"

Ten or twenty years ago, the answer to this question, posed by Patrick McVeigh, of Franklin Research & Development, an investment management firm based in Boston, Massachusetts, was obvious. Large corporations believed that they were impervious to outside influences and that their main function was the preservation of internal employment. But this attitude, so well characterized in John Kenneth Galbraith's *The New Industrial State*, written in 1968, began to change in the early seventies when Ralph Nader launched Project GM, which was designed to force the company to appoint more women and minorities to the board. At the same time concerns about U.S. holdings in South Africa and the implicit support of apartheid began to grow. With those concerns came the beginnings of a new vehicle for casting a vote for change at home and abroad: socially responsible investing (SRI).

SRI investment and research firms "screen" corporate performance in a broad range of areas including women's and family issues; workplace issues; involvement with the defense and nuclear industries; involvement with tobacco, alcohol, and gambling; and environmental responsibility. For example, Franklin Research & Development, one of the earliest SRI firms, publishes a monthly newsletter, *Franklin's Insight* and the *Franklin's Insight Equity Briefs*, which profile companies of interest to a broad range of individual and institutional investors and provide Franklin's Social Assessment Ratings on South African involvement, employee relations, the environment, citizenship, energy, products, and weapons.

All companies today should be aware of the growing influence of SRI because those who screen corporate behavior are paying particular attention to environmental performance now that the "torch" has passed from South Africa to the environment.

SRI is neither a fringe movement nor a passing fad. Anywhere from $625 billion to more than a trillion dollars are invested in screened vehicles. And as "social products" such as mutual funds and pension funds[1] have demonstrated that

---

[1] Social products that involve environmental screens should not be confused with funds and other vehicles that invest in environmental service companies (e.g., companies that manage hazardous waste or provide air quality consulting services, etc). The environmental service sector investments seek to capitalize on the likely growth of companies dealing with remediation of environmental problems and may include firms whose environmental performance is less than exemplary.

they are viable alternatives to traditional investment vehicles,[2] they will likely attract more investors. Although traditional financial wisdom argues against limiting the available universe of potential investments, there is a growing belief that screening out companies that perform poorly based on social criteria also eliminates companies with liabilities that will ultimately affect them financially.

Interestingly, the profile of those placing their money in environmentally screened companies cuts across a variety of political constituencies and social strata. SRI investors range from liberal baby boomers who went to college in the sixties to conservative World War II veterans. Among the latter are people who've hunted and fished since childhood and now find their favorite woods clear-cut or their favorite streams so contaminated that they cannot take home their catch.

The growth of SRI and the corporate research firms that serve this industry represent a new direction in environmental activism. In addition to public protest, legal advocacy, and lobbying for government action, many environmental advocates are choosing to work from within the company as shareholders. Consider Mindy Lubber, founder and president of Green Century Capital Management, Inc., who gained her experience with environmental law while serving with the Public Interest Research Group (PIRG), noted for state and national advocacy in environmental and consumer issues. She views Green Century Capital Management as an important alternative means for solving environmental problems.

[2] By way of comparison, in 1991 the Domini Social Index (see page 184), which tracks the financial performance of 400 major corporations that have passed numerous screens, showed a gain of 37.8 percent. For the same period S&P showed a gain of 30.5 percent. In 1992, DSI rose 12.1 percent, while S&P increased 7.7 percent. The Green Century Balanced Fund (see page 182), founded in March 1992, was number nine in performance on a list of 77 balanced funds, and matched the Micropal Average (a survey of balanced funds) in the six-month period ending October 31, 1992.

"You need to shake at a system in as many ways as possible," asserts Lubber. "Social Funds are important in that they add another tool in the arsenal of advocacy. They can persuade corporations that it is in their best interest to act responsibly." And although some companies may view them as internal irritants, the results of this "oyster strategy" can be genuine pearls in which pressing environmental problems are solved in a fashion that benefits both the company and its stakeholders.

This chapter is designed to help you understand the new environmental activism and the growing popularity of socially responsible investing. It will teach you about SRI and how allied research groups that supply information and stimulate shareholder activism rate major companies in terms of environmental performance. It will also provide guidelines for ensuring that your company receives a fair review and explain how to avoid mistakes when dealing with the SRI and "corporate watchdog" community.

The following pages are divided into five sections. The first discusses entities that either manage investment money for individuals and institutions or provide corporate information for money managers who do. The second discusses companies that profile and track corporate behavior but do not provide investment advice. The third and fourth provide an overview of shareholder activism and entities that focus on organizing boycotts and fostering grass-roots environmental action. All four sections provide a sampling of major companies and groups and discuss how they acquire information and determine corporate ratings. The final section of the chapter discusses how to best work with SRI and corporate research firms so that your company's environmental performance is accurately portrayed.

INVESTMENT ORGANIZATIONS

Today, individual and institutional investors can place their money in numerous social products that include mutual and other funds. The largest group of funds is offered by the Calvert Group of Bethesda, Maryland. Founded in 1976, Calvert now offers more than 20 investment options. Six funds, whose combined portfolios exceed $1 billion, are screened for social and environmentally responsible performance. Four of the six products are grouped under the Calvert Social Investment Fund (CSIF). These include the Money Market Portfolio, Managed Growth Portfolio, Equity Portfolio, and Bond Portfolio. Although the four products have different investment objectives, they share the same social screening criteria. Of course, the financial performance of companies being considered for these portfolios is of primary importance. But once this prerequisite has been met, CSIF sets about evaluating the candidates based on a rigorous set of social standards.

United States Trust Company of Boston (USTC), an asset management firm, helps screen companies for all four portfolios in the Calvert Social Investment Fund. It also makes the investment decisions for three of the funds. In addition to working with Calvert, USTC, founded in 1974 by SRI pioneer Robert Zevin, represents screened investments totalling more than $1 billion.

Kristin Finn, a USTC research analyst, says: "The environmental aspect of screening is gaining popularity. Newer clients are interested primarily in environmental screens. The environmental interest on the part of our clients may be related to some aspect of an organization's interest, such as the Sierra Club Legal Defense Fund. But there are also a growing number of clients who simply want to focus on environment." Finn attributes this burgeoning interest to a growing concern with environmental issues in general as well as a natural extension of other areas of screened investments—as SRI has matured, investors and analysts have broadened the scope of screens being applied to corporate performance.

Like other corporate and SRI research organizations, USTC procures its information from a broad base of resources. In addition to subscribing to the KLD Social Investment database (see page 183) and the Council on Economic Priorities' Corporate Environmental Data Clearinghouse (see page 189), USTC draws on EPA databases, and reviews information from environmental publications, the Department of Justice, and Toxic Release Inventory reports filed under the requirements of the Emergency Planning and Community Right to Know Act. It also relies on material supplied by the companies, such as annual reports and 10-K forms, as well as interviews with key managers.

To evaluate a company for possible recommendation to Calvert or a similar firm, USTC considers performance in the following areas:

- Policy

- Management

- Waste minimization and disposal

- Regulatory compliance

- Energy conservation

- Audits and record-keeping

- Emergency preparedness

- Product (life-cycle analysis)

According to Finn, recommendations to Calvert are based on a blend of qualitative and quantitative information; evaluations factor in the type of industry in which a company operates as well as past environmental performance. Finn notes that although patterns of violations are an important indicator of environmental performance, companies in certain industries can be in full regulatory compliance and not meet acceptable standards of environmental performance. As a result, USTC excludes from evaluation certain types of companies, such as those that operate nuclear power facilities, manufacture pesticides, or produce CFCs.

While maintaining stringent criteria, USTC's evaluations do make allowances for the environmental problems inherent in certain industries; in a sense, the evaluations provide for a kind of environmental "handicap." For example, the paper industry has a long history of water pollution problems that will take considerable technological innovation to remedy. It would therefore be unfair to judge a paper manufacturer that has made good strides to curtail pollution by the same criteria used to evaluate a manufacturer that does not have to create new technology to solve old environmental problems. However, even when the inherent problems of a "dirty" industry are considered, a company must be performing better than the industry average to receive a favorable evaluation.

Currently, USTC does include a paper company in its portfolio: Consolidated Papers in Wisconsin. According to Finn, Consolidated Papers has a good compliance record relative to others in this industry and has improved its environmental disclosure, due in part to a shareholder resolution calling for better reporting on the company's efforts to implement the CERES Principles.

USTC views shareholder activism as an important step in stimulating a dialogue with company decision makers. For example, the firm sponsored a shareholder initiative with Gannett concerning environmental performance reporting. Representatives of USTC and other cosponsors met with management, which agreed to produce an environmental performance report for the shareholders—if the resolution was withdrawn. The sponsors agreed, and Gannett issued the report. Finn notes that the report was not as detailed as USTC had hoped for, but it forced Gannett management to understand that to effectively deal with environmental issues, companies must go beyond mere compliance.

Another company that promotes shareholder activism is Green Century Capital Management, Inc., of Boston, Massachusetts, which manages its own social products, the Green Century Balanced Fund, and the Green Century Money Market Fund. Green Century Capital Management was founded in response to nonprofit environmental organizations seeking investment opportunities for themselves and their members. The Green Century funds are unique in that all of the profits are donated to environmental organizations. Also, as a no-load fund, Green Century is not likely to be promoted by investment brokers, so it relies on connections to nonprofit organizations. This gives Green Century an opportunity to reach environmental activists and institutions as potential investors.

In addition to evaluating environmental performance, Green Century excludes companies from its portfolio based on a variety of social screens including South African investment, tobacco products, nuclear power, and weapons manufacture. Within environmental performance, it examines companies for environmental compliance, packaging, recycling, hazardous materials reduction, and corporate environmental officers, among others.

Like USTC, Green Century believes that it has an important role in influencing the environmental performance of companies in its portfolio. Says Green Century's Mindy Lubber, "We can have more of an impact as advocates in the capital market than as traditional advocates. We see our role as shareholders opening the door for very powerful action."

180

Green Century demonstrated the impact of shareholder action when it learned about an ongoing and illegal release of toxic wastes at the site of a company in its portfolio. The company otherwise had an excellent environmental track record and was considered a "good corporate citizen" in SRI circles. After first learning of the problem from the California Public Interest Research Group, Green Century solicited the help of the National Environmental Law Center (NELC). NELC was able to confirm a violation of the Clean Water Act and subsequently filed suit against the company. At the same time, Green Century contacted the company's CEO, who responded "promptly and appropriately" in addressing the problem. As Lubber points out, "at the level of Fortune 500's, there are some very good and responsible companies—but none of them are perfectly pure and clean." She makes the point that it's often desirable to work with a company and help it improve its performance rather than simply drop them from the portfolio.

USTC and Green Century Management are but two investment organizations that screen companies for environmental performance and take an active role in promoting positive change. Expect more social products to appear in coming years and, as a result, more shareholder activism in the environmental arena. In the next section, we'll look at firms that supply screening information to managers of social products, the media, and environmental advocates.

CORPORATE RESEARCH ORGANIZATIONS

A number of firms provide information to the SRI community in a variety of formats. Consider Kinder, Lydenberg, Domini & Company, Inc. (KLD) of Cambridge, Massachusetts. In addition to being a major supplier of information to the SRI

181

community, KLD offers the Domini 400 Social Index, a market capitalization weighted common stock index of 400 U.S. companies that have met multiple social criteria.

To compile the Domini Index, KLD applied a set of initial screens to the Standard and Poor's 500 Index. This left a subset of 255 companies that demonstrated what KLD deemed acceptable social performance. KLD then added 50 more companies with notable social performance. To reach the desired number of 400, KLD applied the screens to a set of larger companies outside the S&P 500 and selected 95 that offered industry representation or substantial market capitalization while meeting the screening criteria.

The standards used in screening companies for the DSI 400 are both exclusive and inclusive. KLD excludes the following categories from the Domini Social Index:

- Corporations with operations in South Africa, equity interests in companies doing business there, or arrangements that allow the South African government to obtain strategic products.

- Military contractors that supply parts for nuclear weapons or that derive more than 4 percent of gross sales from conventional weapons.

- Firms deriving sales from gambling, distilling alcoholic beverages, or manufacturing tobacco products.

- Companies owning interests in nuclear power plants, operating in the nuclear power industry, or producing any materials directly involved in the nuclear fuel cycle.

- Corporations with notably poor records on the environment, employee relations, or community relations.

KLD seeks to include companies in these categories in the Domini Social Index:

■ Firms that are owned or operated by women or minorities or that have made substantial progress in affirmative hiring or promotion.

■ Enterprises that take a strong stance—backed by action—on the necessity for environmental responsibility; make products useful in maintaining a clean environment; and view energy production processes and consumption in an environmental context.

■ Corporations that make exceptional efforts to treat employees fairly, promote employee involvement, and share ownership or profits with employees.

■ Firms that emphasize the quality of their products and their relationships with consumers and customers.

In addition to maintaining the DSI 400, KLD now offers the Domini Social Index Trust, a no-load mutual fund investing in the common stock of companies included in the Domini Social Index.

While creating the Domini 400 Social Index, KLD gathered extensive data on 1,200 companies and now sells reports on 650 of the companies it evaluated (see Figure 9.1). The reports can be purchased individually or on a subscription basis which includes annual reviews. Another information product that resulted from KLD's work on the Social Index is the KLD Social Investment Database, an online service that provides reviews of more than 800 companies. Subscribers can search companies by various screens and construct model portfolios.

In evaluating companies for environmental performance, KLD considers actions in the following areas:

Areas of Strength

1. The company derives more than 4 percent of revenues from products or services used in cleaning up the environment. (This screen excludes landfill, incineration,

CONSOLIDATED PAPERS, INC.

TICKER	COMMUNITY	EMPLOYEE RELATIONS	ENVIRONMENT	PRODUCT	WOMEN/ MINORITIES	OTHER	MILITARY CONTRACTS	NUCLEAR POWER	SOUTH AFRICA
CPER		X	X	X				XX	
								XX	

AREAS OF STRENGTH AND AREAS OF CONCERN

No Concern =   Concern = X   Major Concern = XX
No Strength =   Strength = X   Major Strength = XX

BUSINESS

Consolidated Paper's primary business is the manufacture and marketing of enamel ("glossy") printing papers (84.6% of 1990 sales). As of 1990, it had approximately 12% of the U.S. market for coated papers. It also produces custom–designed specialty paper, as well as paperboard and corrugated containers. Its 7 plants are in Wisconsin. The company owns 672,000 acres of timberland, approximately half of which is in Canada.

COMMUNITY COMMENTARY

In 1990 the company donated 0.45% ($1 million) in pretax profit to charity.

EMPLOYEE RELATIONS

In an industry where management's relations with unions are often strained, Consolidated's are exceptionally strong. The company stresses open communications. In 1989 its president, Patrick Brennan, held informal breakfasts with all first and second line supervisors in the company over a 6–month period.

As part of its quality programs, the company has adopted a team approach to problem solving throughout its operations. In 1989 and 1991 the firm took the unusual step of making options of company stock available to all nonunion employees.

In 1989 the company created a $5 million Employee Stock Ownership Plan. The company has a defined benefit pension plan and a 401(k) savings plan (with a company match of up to 2.5% of employees' compensation).

ENVIRONMENT

In 1990 the company formed a chlorine reduction advisory committee. As of 1991, it had begun to implement a long-term plan to reduce chlorine use. It currently uses oxygen delignification (bleaching) for the hardwood pulp it produces and is looking into introducing a similar process for its softwood pulp. It is looking into substituting hydrogen peroxide in other stages of the bleaching process. Many environmentalists advocate non-chlorine bleaching as the best way of reducing toxic organcchlorine emissions.

In 1990 the company produced approximately 33,000 tons of 100%–recycled paperboard. In 1990 and 1991, it introduced 3 different grades of recycled enamel papers, but doesn't release figures on the volume of their sales.

In 1990 it published in its quarterly report to shareholders its response to the Valdez Principles. The company asserts that it uses 38% less energy per ton of paper product than the industry average. Like other paper companies, it has made environmentally related land donations. In 1989 it gave 34,600 acres of Minnesota timberlands valued at $4.1 million to the Minnesota Trust for Public Land.

PRODUCT

In 1988 the company instituted a total quality management program which is now companywide. It relies primarily on the Juran quality initiatives. As of 1990, employee teams had approximately 50 production improvement projects underway.

WOMEN AND MINORITIES COMMENTARY

The firm reports that, as of 1989, 15.3% (150 of 975) of its management/supervisory positions were held by women. According to 1989 figures compiled by the U.S. Equal Employment Opportunity Commission, women on average held 8.6% of officials and managers positions at U.S. paper mills.

Factual material is obtained from sources we believe to be reliable, but cannot be guaranteed.

Copyright 1992 Kinder, Lydenberg, Domini, & Co., Inc.

Figure 9.1 Sample Company Review: Kinder, Lydenberg, Domini & Company, Inc. Reprinted with permission.

and deep-well injection services.) Or it has developed innovative products with environmental benefits.

2. The company as a whole has made changes in production processes to minimize or eliminate the use of toxic or hazardous chemicals that make it a leader in its industry.

3. The company is a substantial user of recycled material in its manufacturing processes. Or it is a major factor in the recycling industry.

4. The company derives more than 4 percent of revenues from developing, using, or marketing fuels with environmental advantages. Or it is a major factor in the cogeneration market.

5. The company maintains its property, plant, and equipment with above-average environmental performance for its industry.

Areas of Concern

1. The company's liabilities for hazardous waste disposal sites exceed $30 million or extend to more than 20 Superfund sites. Or the company has Superfund sites at its facilities.

2. The company has recently paid significant fines or civil penalties (over $100,000) or has been involved in major controversies involving some form of environmental degradation.

3. The company is among the top producers or legal emitters of chlorofluorocarbons (CFCs), hydrochlorofluorocarbons (HCFCs), methyl Chloroform, or other ozone-depleting chemicals.

4. The company is among the top legal emitters of toxic chemicals. Or its emissions play a substantial role in the formation of acid rain.

5. The company is a substantial producer of agricultural chemicals (pesticides and chemical fertilizers).

KLD derives information from a variety of sources including more than 200 publications in a variety of fields, online databases, newsletters, government documents, publications from environmental organizations, publications from financial institutes and foundations, interviews with stakeholders, and various corporate documents such as annual reports and 10-K forms. The firm also interviews managers at the companies being reviewed and on rare occasions will conduct a site visit.

According to KLD principal Peter Kinder, the reports "never see the light of day" until KLD has shared them with the company. Kinder notes that including companies in the loop gives them an opportunity to present additional evidence, such as programs or awards that may not have been taken into account, and to present information countering any negative findings in the screened areas.

Companies rated by another major supplier of information to the SRI community, the Council on Economic Priorities (CEP) of New York City, also have the opportunity to review the findings before they are offered to the public. Founded in 1969 by former stockbroker Alice Tepper Marlin (after she received more than 600 responses to an advertisement for a "peace-portfolio"), the Council on Economic Priorities is perhaps best known for its best-selling *Shopping for a Better World* (Ballantine), the 1992 edition of which has more than a million copies in print. The book presents simple checklist ratings on more than 400 companies in 12 areas of social and political concern. A sample page is reproduced in Figure 9.2.

187

Company or Product	Abbr	$	♀	⚥	🖐	🐇	🌿	Y/N	🌲	🏠	🏭	ALERT
Georgia-Pacific	GP	✖	✔	✔	?	✓	✔	No	✖	?	?	clearcutting; on-site day care
Gerber Products	GEB	✓	✔	?	?	✖	?	Yes	?	?	?	D.C.C.A.; infant formula
Gillette	GS	✓	✓	✔	✔⊙	✔	✔	YesIN	✓	✔	✔	
Goya Foods Inc.	GOYA	?	?	?	?	✖	?	No	?	?	?	
Grand Metropolitan PLC	GMP	✓	✔	✔	✔	✔	✔	YesIN	✓	✓	✓	⊕; U.K.
Heinz Company, H.J.	HNZ	✔	✔	✓	✔	✔	✓	No	✔	✔	✓	C.C.A.
Hershey Foods Corp.	HSY	✓	✔	✔	✔*	✔	✔	No	✔	✔	✔	on-site day care
Hormel & Co., George A.	HRL	?	✖	?	✔	✖	?	No	?	?	?	
Int'l Res. & Dev. Corp.	IRDV	?	✖	?	✖○	✖	?	No	?	?	?	
James River Corporation	JR	✓	✖	✓	✖	✔	✓	No	✖	✓	✓	on-site day care
John B. Sanfilippo, Inc.	JSAN	?	?	?	✔	✖	?	No	?	?	?	
Johnson & Johnson	JNJ	✔	✔	✔	✔⊙	✔	✔	YesIN	✔	✔	✔	on-site day care; Workplace Principles
Johnson, S.C. & Son	SCJ	✔+	✔	✔	✔*	✔	✔	YesIN	✔	✔	✔	1st to ban CFCs; on-site day care
Johnson Products Co.	JPC	?	✓	✔	✖	✖	?	No	?	?	?	
Kellogg Company	K	✔	✔	✔	✔*	✔	✔	YesIN	✔	✔	✔	C.C.A.
Kimberly-Clark Corp.	KMB	?	✔	✔	✖	✖	?	YesIN	✖	?	?	disposable diapers
L'Oreal S.A.	LORA	?	✔	✓	✔*	✓	?	Yes	?	?	?	
Land O' Lakes Inc.	LAND	✔+	✔	✔	?	✔	✓	No	✓	✔	✓	co-op
Marcal Paper Mills Inc.	MARC	?	✓	✖	✔	✓	✔	No	✔	?	?	
Mars, Inc.	MARS	?	?	?	?	✓	?	No	?	✔	?	
McCormick & Co., Inc.	MCRK	✔	✖	?	✔	✖	?	No	?	?	?	
Mead Corporation	MEA	?	✓	✓	?	✓	?	No	✓∅	✓	✓	
Melitta Bentz KG	MTA	?	?	✔	✔	✔	✔	No	✔	✔	✓	
Minn. Mining & Mfg. (3M)	MMM	✓	✔	✔	✔*	✔	✔	YesIN	✓	✔	✔	❅

✔ = Top Rating   ✓ = Middle Rating   ✖ = Bottom Rating   ? = Insufficient Information   Page 109
For a more detailed explanation see key on page 14

LARGE COMPANIES

Figure 9.2 Page sample from *Shopping for a Better World* (Used with permission by the Council on Economic Priorities)

Although CEP does not serve as a financial advisor, it does provide information to organizations such as USTC and Green Century Capital Management. CEP is best described as a non-profit information resource on corporate environmental behavior. Its staff uses a variety of publications, online databases, government sources, toxic release reports, and questionnaires sent to companies under review to update *Shopping for a Better World* and a companion book, *The Better World Investment Guide*, published by Prentice Hall.

In addition to compiling the two books, CEP offers the Institutional Investor Research Service (IIRS) and the Corporate Environmental Data Clearinghouse (CEDC). IIRS tracks and issues monthly reports on more than 200 publicly held companies, offering ratings in the following areas:

- Environment

- South African investment

- Women's advancement

- Minority advancement

- Military contracts

- Charitable giving

- Animal testing

- Disclosure of information

- Community outreach

- Family benefits

- Workplace issues

CEP's Corporate Environmental Data Clearinghouse, launched in April 1990, consists of information on the overall environmental performance of Standard & Poor's 500 companies. The reports (70 of which are available at the time of this writing) are available to environmentally concerned citizens, nonprofit organizations, investors, and public officials on a sliding fee scale.

189

CEP is an exemplar of the new environmental activism; it has worked closely with trade associations to promote cooperation and the sharing of information in the hopes of resolving pressing environmental and social problems. For example, the American Paper Institute (API), which has not had a particularly warm relationship with environmental critics, worked with CEP after the Council sent its first round of environmental questionnaires to paper companies. With the support of the API, the Council was able to get a considerably higher response rate.

The response of the API is a good indication of the growing acceptance of SRI by corporations. In the interest of encouraging even higher responses and corporate reporting on environmental performance, CEP is working with CERES to develop standardized questionnaires.

The largest and first U.S.–based investment research organization is the Investor Responsibility Research Center Inc. (IRRC), a not-for-profit research center established in 1972 by Harvard University, the Ford Foundation, and other institutions seeking objective information about social and long-term economic aspects of their portfolio investments. IRRC operates five services staffed by specialists that monitor South African business, Corporate Governance, Social Policy Issues such as maquiladoras, defense contracting, tobacco marketing, Global Shareholder issues, and corporate environmental performance. More than 400 institutions and 100 corporations subscribe to one or more IRRC service. (Unlike KLD or CEP, IRRC does not make any investment or product recommendations.)

IRRC's Environmental Information Service is designed to provide investors with a systematic basis for comparing or screening the environmental management and performance of all S&P 500 companies. IRRC subscribers receive an annually updated notebook containing standardized two page profiles of every corporation in the S&P 500 index. See Figure 9.3 for a sample corporate profile. To assure comparability, IRRC's Corporate Environmental Profile Directory provides industry averages for each S&P 500 industry classification. IRRC's environmental staff analyze government data on environmental infractions, oil spills, chemical spills, and hazardous waste liabilities by S&P 500 corporations and their 10,000 plus subsidiaries under 11 environmental laws. To allow analysts to track which companies are able to reduce their environmental burdens more efficiently, IRRC staff developed the IRRC Emissions Efficiency Index and IRRC Environmental Compliance index to compare the environmental emissions and compliance penalties produced along with each unit of revenue.

IRRC's Directory also includes a brief summary of financially or environmentally relevant articles that appeared in either an environmental journal or a major business periodical or online news service. In addition to this quantitative information, the Corporate Environmental Profile Directory gives environmental management information such as the name of the senior corporate environmental official, the size of a company's environmental staff, the name of the board committee responsible for environmental affairs, the frequency of environmental audits performed by the company, and the company's most important environmental projects. Companies always review each profile, thus improving their accuracy.

In addition to publishing the Directory, Investor's Environmental Report, and periodic studies of issues such as global climate change, ozone depletion, and tropical deforestation, IRRC operates a consortium of institutions that meet quarterly to discuss issues associated with integrating environmental information into their investment activities.

In addition to providing subscribers with profiles, IRRC publishes a bimonthly newsletter, *Investor's Environmental Report*, which focuses on companies' responses to major environ-

ABCD Paper Co.

Paper & Forest Products

Completed IRRC Survey: **Yes**

Environmental Staff

Senior officer:	**Albert Drew**
Title:	**VP, Env., Health & Safety**
Reports to:	**Exec. VP, Legal & External Affairs**
Env. staff:	**50**

Corporate Policy

Board committee: **Environment, Health & Safety**

Directors: **6**
Outside codes: **APAI**

[✔] Env. factor in comp. [✔] Env. Policy
[✔] U.S. Stds. overseas [✔] Env. TQM

Environmental Auditing

Auditing program:	**Yes, as of 1989**
U.S. facilities audited:	**20%**
Non-U.S. facilities audited:	
Avg. time between audits:	**1–2 years**
Conducted by:	**Plant staff, Corp. Staff, Consultants**

Secondary Industries
Nonmetallic minerals, except fuels; Chemicals & allied products; Wholesale trade-durable goods

1991 Proxy Activity
Sign Valdez (4.5%)

Environmental Communication

Methods:	**Ann. rep., 10-K, Shareholder mtg., Press rel.**
Audits available:	**No**
Insurance:	**Third party ($200M sudden & accidental)**

Expenses disclosed:
[✓] Capital [ ] Legal [ ] Contingencies
[ ] O&M [ ] Insurance [ ] Total

Environmental Achievements

- Achieved 75% dioxin reduction in bleached pulp and effluent, 1992.
- Solid waste reduction: 30% year end 1991 with goal of 50% reduction by 1994.
- Environmental audits (self audits and corporate audits) initiated in 1989.
- Introduction of recycled fiber in printing and writing papers.
- Wildlife enhancement projects on company timberlands.

Current Environmental Projects

	Capital Exp.	Target Date
• Further reduction of dioxin at bleach facilities.	$58M	1991–1995
• Solid waste site closures.	$72M	1991–1995
• Pollution prevention; 33% reduction by 1992, 50% by 1995.	–	1992–1995
Deinking facility for recycling newsprint.	$200M	1992–1995

News & Notes

On May 12, 1991, ABCD Paper was sentenced to pay a $1.2 million fine for violation of the Resource Conservation and Recovery Act (RCRA) at its paper mill in Wichita, Kansas. According to the state attorney general, the company generated, stored and treated hazardous waste without a permit and made false statements to federal and state environmental officials. In addition to the fine, a consent decree requires ABCD to monitor and analyze the environmental impact of the plant's discharges. (*ER* 7/21/91; *EW* 7/14/91)

The company announced that it would accept the Coalition of Northeastern Governors' challenge to the nation's 200 largest makers of consumer packaging to reduce volumes of solid waste generated by their packaging (*WSJ* 3/21/91)

The company produces recycled printing and writing papers as well as recycled kraft for paper bags. ABCD is licensing a paper recycling technology from the Germany company PTS GmbH, and is currently constructing a $91 million deinking facility in western New York, to process 260 million tons of used newspapers and magazines per day. (*WSJ* 5/13/91; **company**)

The company contributed $100,000 to the Nature Conservancy, a non-profit organization that purchases land to protect the habitats of rare species, to help preserve Big Eddy Creek in Virginia. (*F* 4/6/90)

Company Comments

Figure 9.3 IRRC Corporate Environmental Profile

Paper & Forest Products   (14 companies)   **ABCD Paper Co.**   (ABCD)

Company 10-K Information Summary

	Environmental Capital Expenditures Actual	Projected	Government Proceedings	Other Legal Proceedings
1987	$43 M	$57 M (1988)	none disclosed	none disclosed
1988	$62 M	$95 M (1989)	1	none disclosed
1989	$88 M	$110 M (1990)	1	1

Government Agency Information Summary

Hazardous Waste Cleanup Responsibilities	Company	Industry Avg.
Superfund NPL sites:	17	6
Parent company NPL sites:	5	4
Subsidiary NPL sites:	12	2
RCRA Corrective Actions required:	6	1
Number of RCRA permit denials, 1987-1990:	1	0

Toxic Chemical Releases

Year	Reported Releases (lbs.)	Annual Revenues	IRRC Emissions Efficiency Index™ Company	Industry Avg.
1988	45,807,560	$10,222 M	4.48	3.25
1989	35,416,630	$12,345 M	2.87	2.52
TOTAL	81,224,190	$22,567 M	3.60	2.87

Reported Spills

Year	Oil Spills > 10,000 gal. Number	Amount (gal.)	Chemical Spills > 10,000 lbs. Number	Amount (lbs.)	Industry Avg. Number of Spills Oil	Chemical
1987	0	0	1	30,077	0	1
1988	0	0	4	213,117	0	1
1989	0	0	2	71,429	0	2

Compliance Data

Statute	Year	Consent Decrees	Number of Penalties Company	Industry Avg.	Total Value of Penalties Company	Industry Avg.	Penalty Indices Company	Industry Avg.
RCRA	1987	0	1	0	14,500	26,429	1.51	6.35
	1988	0	0	0	0	8,107	0.00	1.68
	1989	0	3	0	132,808	13,208	10.76	2.56
CAA	1987	0	3	1	80,400	50,598	8.38	12.16
	1988	0	0	1	0	30,846	0.00	6.40
	1989	1	1	1	900,000	105,950	72.90	20.57
CWA	1987	0	1	0	170,000	15,214	17.71	3.66
	1988	0	0	0	0	1,786	0.00	0.37
	1989	0	1	0	15,000	14,286	1.22	2.77
SDWA	1987	0	0	0	0	0	0.00	0.00
	1988	0	0	0	0	0	0.00	0.00
	1989	0	0	0	0	0	0.00	0.00
TSCA/ FIFRA	1987	0	0	0	0	460	0.00	0.11
	1988	0	1	1	16,200	7,892	1.58	1.64
	1989	0	0	0	0	3,063	0.00	0.59
OSHA	1987	0	8	1	18,935	1,864	1.97	0.45
	1988	0	20	4	75,520	6,539	7.39	1.36
	1989	0	14	9	7,350	11,558	0.60	2.24
AEA	1987	0	0	0	0	0	0.00	0.00
	1988	0	0	0	0	107	0.00	0.02
	1989	0	0	0	0	89	0.00	0.02
MSHA	1987	0	0	0	0	0	0.00	0.00
	1988	0	0	0	0	0	0.00	0.00
	1989	0	0	0	0	0	0.00	0.00
							IRRC Compliance Index™	
TOTAL	1987	0	13	3	283,835	94,565	29.57	22.73
	1988	0	21	6	91,720	55,277	8.97	11.46
	1989	1	19	11	1,055,158	148,153	85.47	28.76
GRAND TOTAL		1	53	20	1,430,713	297,995	44.48	21.08

II-625

Figure 9.3 *(Continued)*

mental problems as well as how investors are taking environmental concerns into their portfolio management activities. For example, one issue describes how corporate buying habits are changing to include environmental considerations. The article cited AT&T's policy to use 100 percent biodegradable packaging for its consumer telephones and answering machines.

Other IRRC information products include the Corporate Governance Service, the Social Issues Service, and the Global Shareholder Service. In addition, IRRC offers ProxyVoter, a software program that enables subscribers to manage their proxy voter responsibilities. Finally, IRRC offers the South Africa Review Service, which provides expert analysis of trends and events, updates on laws in the United States that effect companies doing business in South Africa, and a comprehensive list of those companies.

Jon Naimon, Corporate Program Manager at IRRC, says that "numerous corporations have also subscribed to IRRC's Environmental Information Service because their environmental departments recognize that they need hard environmental information to form the basis for assessments of their environmental programs in comparison with their competitors. These subscriptions represent a new level of commitment among companies, since they are also using the information internally to improve their environmental programs."

While other organizations provide information on corporate behavior, they take similar approaches to those used by the above entities. They represent a concerted effort by professional researchers and evaluators and should be considered serious influences in the investment community. The next section describes organizations designed primarily to induce change from within through aggressive shareholder activism and from without through consumer boycotts.

SHAREHOLDER ACTIVISM

As described previously, some SRI investment organizations practice shareholder activism as a means of solving environmental problems within portfolio companies. The pioneer of this strategy is the Interfaith Center on Corporate Responsibility (ICCR) of New York City. At ICCR, shareholder activism is regarded as a primary tool for influencing corporate behavior, with 80 or more resolutions submitted each year. The ICCR is a coalition of religious groups working to reflect the ideological values of its membership in investment decisions and activism. In pursuing these goals, ICCR relies on resolutions, dialogue with management, divestment, special reports, selective purchasing, and, if nothing else works, consumer boycotts. Shareholder resolutions are often their most effective tool.

Dr. Ariane van Buren, director of Energy and Environmental Programs at ICCR, says: "Shareholders always have the legal right to speak to companies about issues and policies. Although companies can be unresponsive, a well-written stockholder resolution, on the other hand, may have a specific schedule that the company must follow. As a result, companies generally prefer to prevent resolutions from ending up on the proxy table—they try to negotiate a settlement first."

ICCR reports that investors challenged more than 100 corporations on the environmental impact of their products and operations in 1992. The results? Some companies comply. Since Sun Oil endorsed the CERES principles, other major corporations are looking into how public accountability can become advantageous to them. Still there are many who "look no further than the bottom-line quarterly profit," says van Buren. "They resist shareholder requests for long-term environmental accountability. Other companies paint themselves green and assume they can quell skepticism with public re-lations campaigns of slick commercials and glossy reports. These companies are behind the times, and the public isn't buying it."

To move companies into acceptable settlements (that is, find-a-reasonable-solution mode), ICCR's people speak as shareholders. Van Buren explains: "Companies historically re-sist outside interference. But they seem receptive to getting input from shareholders. In addition, more shareholders are recognizing relation between environmental performance and profitability."

Van Buren also stresses that as a coalition of shareholder activists, ICCR does not act as an independent assessor. Efforts to challenge a company about its environmental performance claims focus on the environmental realities witnessed locally around company facilities and operations. Also, it looks for evidence concerning a company's willingness to be publicly accountable. Toward this end, ICCR has exerted significant efforts to further the understanding and acceptance of the CERES Principles (see Chapter 1) through resolutions and meetings with corporate leaders.

ICCR efforts are not limited to environmental issues. The organization is actively involved in areas such as international health, South African investment, equality, Northern Ireland, and the *maquiladoras* industry in Mexico, among others. The ICCR newsletter, *The Corporate Examiner*, published ten times per year, issues updates on resolutions and other activities.

BOYCOTT/GRASS-ROOTS ORGANIZATIONS

In addition to ICCR, leaders of companies today should be aware of two other organizations dedicated to bringing about changes in corporate environmental responsibilities. The first,

Co-op America, channels consumer power in the same way that the SRI movement channels investor power. The *Co-op America Quarterly* magazine includes *Boycott Action News (BAN)* as part of its information for consumers. *BAN* reports on boycotts called by other organizations and attempts to present conflicting information. The fall 1992 newsletter, for example, included a boycott called by Environmental Action against so-called degradable plastics. The listing included where to send for a list of specific products and background articles. The same issue included responses to earlier boycott calls from officials at Ford, Adidas, Mitsubishi Motors, and United Way of America as well as detailed background articles on new boycotts. *BAN* also regularly includes responses from corporations on particular boycotts as well as information from research organization such as IRRC and CEP.

Finally, at the grass-roots level, consider the actions of Citizens Clearinghouse for Hazardous Waste (CCHW). Founded in 1981 by Love Canal activist Lois Gibbs, CCHW is dedicated to building strong community-based environmental organizations. CCHW staff and volunteers provide organizational and technical assistance to activists in local communities dealing with corporations on environmental issues. They accomplish their goal through the dissemination of information about specific corporations as well as general guidebooks and reports. In addition, CCHW provides on-site support designed to help local groups better understand the nature and extent of toxic release and hazardous waste problems.

A key element in CCHW's program is a database of information on corporate environmental performance. By drawing on resources from more than 7,000 local community groups, as well as by sharing information with other national organizations such as Greenpeace, CCHW has amassed considerable information on specific, local environmental practices of major corporations. In some cases, CCHW will issue a summary report detailing the environmental record of a particular company or industry, available at cost to concerned individuals. In addition, CCHW offers technical reports on a range of toxic materials issues.

Although CCHW's goals do not include advocacy or direct influence on corporate behavior, the organization does support grass-roots efforts and provides people in local communities with the information and technical resources they require to confront corporations doing business in their own backyards.

WORKING WITH SRI AND CORPORATE RESEARCH GROUPS

No one can predict how many new SRI and corporate research organizations will emerge in the coming years. Nevertheless, leaders of companies today should count on the level of scrutiny increasing as current companies refine their research methodologies and attract new individual and institutional investors. The preceding sections have given you a sense of the range of organizations that rate major companies and influence potential investors (for an exhaustive review of SRI groups, consult *The Social Investment Almanac*, Holt, 1992). Add to them the popular press, mainstream environmental groups, and the local communities in which you do business, and you have a formidable and knowledgeable constituency that can indeed have an impact on your bottom line. It's up to you whether these watchdogs and factions will become pure adversaries or potential resources to help you improve your performance, your bottom line, and your rating on corporate citizenship.

The following guidelines will help you work with an SRI

or corporate research group if your company is being evaluated; they will also help you prepare for evaluations in the future.

1. Treat SRI and corporate research groups as potential allies. If your company has a solid environmental track record, SRI and corporate research organizations will help inform the investment community about your efforts. You will get the best results if you respond quickly to any inquiries.

You will also find that reporting on environmental performance will be a positive experience in terms of collecting and organizing internal information. It will also help you identify areas in need of shoring up and areas of strength that can serve as foundations for further growth.

2. Give SRI and corporate research groups serious respect. As we've stressed in this book, environmental issues are not simply an "end-of-the-pipe" issue. If you regard them as just another set of regulations or a nuisance to be handled at a fairly low level, you may well find your company negatively portrayed in the press and among environmental groups. Similarly, if you're contacted by an SRI or corporate research organization for information that will be used in a review or evaluation, don't send the researcher or inquiry off to your public relations department. Consider it an opportunity to describe your company's earnest efforts and positive results in the environmental arena, one that should be dealt with by an officer who has high-level authority.

You might also consider creating an ad hoc team of managers to help compile information that can be presented to investigating organizations. Each member of the team should be responsible for maintaining up-to-date information in his or her area of responsibility and for organizing that information in a fashion that will be useful to SRI and corporate researchers.

Finally, treat investors inquiring about your environmental performance in the same way you would treat financial analysts. Pay close attention to the type of information your company passes along to an investigating organization and remember that you will be working with sophisticated researchers with extensive backgrounds in environmental affairs. Grandiose statements of intent or nebulous platitudes won't earn high marks. Be prepared to discuss facts and figures and to document genuine achievements.

3. **Don't solicit reviews.** Peter Kinder of KLD reports that as SRI became more accepted, several companies contacted him requesting a review for their companies. According to Kinder, KLD will never undertake a review at a company's request; it only conducts a special evaluation when requested by one of its clients. Most other SRI and corporate research groups have similar policies.

You can, however, request information on standards from various SRI groups and use them as a basis for forming your own in-house audits. The advantage of this is twofold. First, you'll introduce a set of evaluation criteria that exceed compliance levels. (All of the major SRI and corporate research organizations strongly support CERES—see Chapter 1.) And in the environmental performance arena, people and programs improve as you up the ante. Second, if you are reviewed by an SRI or corporate research organization, you'll have already identified areas of weakness and taken appropriate measures to correct problems. This will increase your chances of securing a favorable rating.

4. **Present solid evidence to redress errors and omissions.** SRI and corporate research organizations want your firm to participate in the review process. If you receive a negative report or a report with ratings that you feel are unjustified, present the investigating organizations with credible

supporting material. Show how you derived your numbers, the circumstances surrounding citations or lawsuits, and so on.

A related issue concerns prior environmental problems. Most companies with any kind of history began doing business in an era when standards of environmental performance were lower than they are today. Don't try to deny past environmental difficulties; rather, demonstrate what you've done to resolve them or outline in detail what you will do in the future to correct them.

5. **Turn shareholder activism to your advantage.** Individuals and organizations involved in drafting resolutions bring to the table a fresh viewpoint, technical expertise, and considerable commitment. Remember, they're not there to sabotage you—they're trying to help you improve the performance of their investment.

In most cases, shareholder activists would choose to negotiate a settlement rather than proceed with a resolution. Take the opportunity to work with them for substantive results. As two decades of strong shareholder activism on issues from South African involvement to employee rights prove, shareholders will continue to press for their causes until some kind of satisfactory results are achieved.

6. **Incorporate SRI and corporate research groups into your sphere of customers.** In Chapter 2, we described how Total Quality Environmental Management focuses on the customer. We also described why, in the case of environmental issues, it is necessary to expand the conception of "customer" to include regulators and critics. If you treat SRI and corporate research organizations like customers, your practice of TQEM will best position you to gain a favorable rating.

Are investment and research organizations having an impact on corporate environmental behavior? Kristin Finn believes that corporations are paying organizations like United

States Trust Company of Boston more heed. "Today, more companies are interested in the results of their evaluations," she says. "One indication is that a few years ago, it was tough to get past the PR person at the companies we were researching. Now, we have a much better chance of getting directly to the environmental manager." Peter Kinder of Kinder, Lyndenberg, Domini & Company echoes Finn's assessments: "When we began in 1988, we couldn't get people to return our phone calls. Now, we have companies falling all over themselves to talk to us. Corporate America is finally beginning to understand that organizations like ours serve as proxies for a much larger group of investors. They're beginning to understand that we really represent a political movement. To use the phrase of political scientist and professor David Vogel of the University of California, Berkeley, what we're doing is 'lobbying corporations.' "

KNOW THE UNIVERSE OF ENVIRONMENTAL WATCHDOGS

1. Your financial future will be closely related to your environmental performance; an increasing number of investors use environmental performance and related criteria to determine which companies they support.

2. We are in the midst of a new era of environmental activism, in which environmental advocates work from within to initiate change. An adversarial approach to those seeking change will never work to your advantage.

3. Substantiate claims, document your achievements, and be honest about past problems.

4. Consider the evaluation process as a learning tool. Use it as a way to improve your performance—could you complete an evaluation today and expect a satisfactory rating? Learn what their criteria are.

5. Ultimately, there is only one way to guarantee a sustained "nod of green approval": develop, demonstrate, and maintain excellence in all aspects of environmental performance.

EPILOGUE

ENVIRONMENTAL CHALLENGES FOR TWENTY-FIRST CENTURY COMPANIES

Can we balance economic growth with protection of our natural environment? The acrimony this topic generated in the 1992 presidential debates made it clear that there is no pat answer. We are optimistic, however, and believe that businesses are at the threshold of a unique opportunity to lead a concerted effort that will halt and reverse much of the environmental decline brought about in the age of industrialization. We also believe that companies taking a leadership role in environmental affairs now will be at the forefront of new growth opportunities in the years ahead.

To do their share, corporations will not only have to address the kind of problems described in the preceding pages but will also have to consider the following challenges during the remainder of the decade:

1. **Pressure to report a "double bottom line."** In Chapter 1, we presented the "double bottom line"—one that includes environmental performance—as a vanguard concept. But as we demonstrated in Chapter 9, watchdog and social responsibility groups have brought awareness of environmental performance to the forefront. Companies that ignore the importance of environmental behavior will experience far more than a "PR crisis"; their ability to attract shareholders, customers, and future employees will be at stake. To meet the reporting demands of the future, the leaders of today's business organizations will have to adopt a new mentality, one in which environmental factors are given the same weight as traditional cost factors in determining how products are made and profits are determined. In short, traditional accounting methods will have to be supplemented by an approach that considers the short- and long-term impact of environmental factors.

2. **Increased R&D demands.** Many of today's solid waste and pollution problems are being addressed by rethinking old ways of manufacturing and packaging products. But in the years ahead, basic engineering and production approaches will have to include "total life-cycle" and design-for-environment considerations. That in turn will require new materials and production processes and an investment of research and development funds. Initially, this will be a painful expenditure for many companies because the payoff is one that will not directly show up on the corporate books. Companies that invest R&D in the environment will, however, reap benefits by avoiding costly problems and regulatory requirements in the future.

3. **Growing internal pressure.** As we stressed in Chapter
   4 and elsewhere in this book, many employees today
   are modifying their behaviors with regard to recycling
   and the disposal of household hazardous wastes and have
   factored environmental quality into their purchasing decisions. They also want to see changes in the workplace
   that reflect their environmental concerns.

   The next generation of employees will have even
   stronger sentiments. Today, as early as preschool, children across the country are learning the importance of
   recyling and taking positive environmental actions. Tomorrow, when they enter the workforce, they'll expect
   their employers to provide the tools and systems necessary to be environmentally responsible. They'll also
   expect their employers to demonstrate a genuine commitment to doing the "right thing" independently of the
   positive PR and marketing benefits that corporate environmental action affords.

4. **A more educated and vocal public.** As we described
   in Chapter 7, some environmental organizations now
   view corporations as a vehicle for cleaning up and preventing pollution and are willing to work with business
   towards a common goal. But that shift from the "adversary model" to the "partner model" has yet to filter
   down to the general public. Numerous polls indicate that
   many people consider corporations to be responsible for
   the state of the environment and unwilling to solve the
   problems they've created. Many people also regard the
   environmental actions of corporations to be thinly veiled
   attempts to jump on the "green bandwagon" and exploit
   a national interest.

   Eventually, the sincere efforts and tangible accomplishments of corporate America will change attitudes.

But in the meantime, the business community is fighting an uphill battle. By putting into practice the principles described in this book and maintaining open, honest, and accurate channels of communication, businesses can pave the way for more trust and better relations. The old adage, "actions speak louder than words," rings true when it comes to environmental responsibility.

5. **New regulatory hurdles.** Not many people are willing to let companies regulate their own environmental behavior (refer to Chapter 5). As a result of voter pressure, local, state, and federal lawmakers will increasingly respond to demands for a safer, cleaner environment. As the early nineties have proven, the states are often the quickest to respond to calls for environmental action. And until federal laws catch up, companies face the prospect of creating multiple versions of products to satisfy a potentially conflicting web of individual state laws.

The increasing involvement of states in the regulatory process will create challenges for an ever-larger segment of the business community. In the past, environmental legislation applied primarily to large concerns that used or created toxic substances or made significant contributions to air and water pollution. Today, corner dry cleaners and paint shops in the Los Angeles area must comply with stringent laws. Tomorrow, manufacturers and distributors will have to consider packaging strategies and options that enable them to comply with laws in various regions of the country as states and municipalities confront the solid waste disposal crisis with hard-hitting legislation.

6. **New information demands.** As Kathryn Fuller of the

World Wildlife Fund has said: "Successful companies in the twenty-first century will be those best able to secure public confidence. That means in part a progressive policy on the public release and scrutiny of environmental information. All too often, 'commercial confidentiality' is used as a blanket excuse to arbitrarily limit release of information which belongs in the public domain. Open access to information should be the rule, with restrictions justified—not vice versa."

"We needed authorization. As an oil company we can't just go out and start [cleaning up]," commented Lawrence Rawl of Exxon Corporation as an excuse for why his company delayed cleanup actions for two days following the Valdez oil spill. Don't wait; no company needs authorization to strive for environmental excellence.

Appendix

BUSINESS AND ENVIRONMENT RESOURCE GUIDE

MAJOR ENVIRONMENTAL ORGANIZATIONS

World Wildlife Fund
1250 24th Street NW
Washington, D.C. 20037
(202) 293-4800 (Public information)
FAX (202) 293-9211
Over 1.2 million members
Focus: Wildlife

National Wildlife Federation
1400 16th Street NW
Washington, D.C. 20036

(202) 797-6800
FAX (703) 790-4040
(800) 822-9919 (Customer service for National Wildlife)
(800) 432-6564 (Membership)
(202) 797-6857 (HQ/Public information)
5.3 million members
Focus: Natural resources

Nature Conservancy
1815 N. Lynn Street
Arlington, VA 22209
(703) 841-5300
FAX (703) 841-1283
Mails annual report
645 members
Focus: Purchasing land for endangered species, ecosystems,
and plant life

National Audubon Society
950 Third Avenue
New York, NY 10022
(212) 832-3200
FAX (212) 644-5742
Focus: To affect public policies regarding endangered species,
pollution, wildlife

Sierra Club
730 Polk Street
San Francisco, CA 94109
(415) 776-2211
FAX (415) 776-0350
625,000 members

Wilderness Society
900 17th Street NW
Washington, D.C. 20006
(202) 833-2300
FAX (202) 429-3958
317,000 members
Focus: Conservation and protection of wildlife and lands

Environmental Defense Fund
257 Park Avenue S
New York, NY 10010
(212) 505-2100
FAX (212) 505-0892
200,000+ members
Focus: Links science, economics, and law to create innovative solutions to environmental problems; first major battle won was the ban of the pesticide DDT

Center for Science in the Public Interest
1875 Connecticut Avenue NW, Suite 300
Washington, D.C. 20009
(202) 332-9110
FAX (202) 265-4954
266,000 members
Focus: Consumer advocate group specializing in nutrition

Clean Water Action
1320 18th Street NW, Suite 300
Washington, D.C. 20036
(202) 457-1286
FAX (202) 457-0287
Focus: Lobbying, litigation for clean water, environmental issues; national level

Greenpeace
1436 U Street NW
Washington, DC 20009
(202) 462-1177
Focus: Atmosphere, energy, toxics, tropical rainforests

National Geographic Society
1145 17th Street NW
Washington, D.C. 20036
(202) 857-7000
10 million + members
Focus: Conservation; geographic educational materials, magazines, books, globes

National Parks and Conservation Association
1776 Massachusetts Avenue NW
Washington, D.C. 20036
(202) 223-6722
FAX (202) 659-0650
308,000 members
Annual budget: $4 million
Focus: A nonprofit citizen member organization focused on the preservation and protection of national parks

National Resources Defense Council
40 W. 20th Street
New York, NY 10011
(212) 727-2700
FAX (212) 727-1773
175,000+ members
Focus: Natural resources, rain forests, conservation, pesticides

Union of Concerned Scientists
26 Church Street
Cambridge, MA 02238
(617) 547-5552
FAX (617) 864-9405
100,000+ members
Focus: Energy and arms control, environmental warming, nuclear issues

U.S. Public Interest Research Group
215 Pennsylvania Avenue SE
Washington, D.C. 20003
(202) 546-9707
FAX (202) 546-2461
1.2 million members
Focus: Environmental and consumer issues; toxics, air pollution

FEDERAL AGENCIES

U.S. Department of Energy
1000 Independence Avenue SW
Washington, D.C. 20585
(202) 586-5000

U.S. Department of Energy
Office of Industrial Technologies
1000 Independence Avenue SW
Room 6B052
Washington, D.C. 20585
(202) 586-9232

U.S. Department of Energy
Office of Transportation Technologies
1000 Independence Avenue SW
Room 6B094
Washington, D.C. 20585
(202) 586-8594

U.S. Department of Energy
Office of Utilities Technologies
1000 Independence Avenue SW
Room 6C036
Washington, D.C. 20585
(202) 586-9275

U.S. Department of Energy
Office of Building Technologies
1000 Independence Avenue SW
Room 6A081
Washington, D.C. 20585
(202) 586-1510
Focus: Codes and standards

U.S. Department of Energy
Office of Technology and Financial Assistance
1000 Independence Avenue SW
Room 6A049
Washington, D.C. 20585
(202) 586-9240

U.S. Environmental Protection Agency
Main Administration
401 M Street SW
Washington, D.C. 20460
(202) 260-4700

U.S. Environmental Protection Agency
Office of International Activities
401 M Street SW
Room W1135
Washington, D.C. 20460
(202) 260-4870

U.S. Environmental Protection Agency
Administration and Resources Management
401 M Street SW
Room W1111
Washington, D.C. 20460
(202) 260-4600

U.S. Environmental Protection Agency
Enforcement
401 M Street SW
Room W1037
Washington, D.C. 20460
(202) 260-4134

U.S. Environmental Protection Agency
Office of General Counsel
401 M Street SW
Room W537
Washington, D.C. 20460
(202) 260-8067

U.S. Environmental Protection Agency
Office of Policy, Planning and Evaluation
401 M Street SW
Room W1013
Washington, D.C. 20460
(202) 260-4332

U.S. Environmental Protection Agency
Office of the Inspector General
401 M Street SW
Room NE3071
Washington, D.C. 20460
(202) 260-3137

U.S. Environmental Protection Agency
Water
401 M Street SW
Room E1035
Washington, D.C. 20460
(202) 260-5700

U.S. Environmental Protection Agency
Solid Waste and Emergency Response
401 M Street SW
Room SE360
Washington, D.C. 20460
(202) 260-4610

U.S. Environmental Protection Agency
Air and Radiation
401 M Street SW
Room W937
Washington, D.C. 20460
(202) 260-7400

U.S. Environmental Protection Agency
Prevention, Pesticides, and Toxic Substances
401 M Street SW
Room E637
Washington, D.C. 20460
(202) 260-2902

U.S. Environmental Protection Agency
Office of Research and Development
401 M Street SW
Room W913
Washington, D.C. 20460
(202) 260-7676

U.S. Department of the Interior
1849 C Street NW
Washington, D.C. 20240
(202) 208-3100
FAX (202) 208-5048

U.S. Department of the Interior
National Parks Service
1849 C Street NW
Washington, D.C. 20240
(202) 208-7394

U.S. Department of the Interior
Fish and Wildlife Service
1849 C Street NW
Washington, D.C. 20240
(202) 208-5634

U.S. Department of the Interior
Office of Environmental Affairs
1849 C Street NW
Washington, D.C. 20240
(202) 208-2024

U.S. Department of the Interior
U.S. Geological Survey
1849 C Street NW

Washington, D.C. 20240
(703) 648-4460

U.S. Department of the Interior
Bureau of Mines
1849 C Street NW
Washington, D.C. 20240
(202) 501-9649

U.S. Department of the Interior
Bureau of Reclamation
1849 C Street NW
Washington, D.C. 20240
(202) 208-4662

U.S. Department of the Interior
Minerals Management Service
1849 C Street NW
Washington, D.C. 20240
(202) 208-3983

U.S. Department of the Interior
Bureau of Land Management
1849 C Street NW
Washington, D.C. 20240
(202) 208-5717

Executive Office of the President
Council on Environmental Quality
722 Jackson Place NW
Washington, D.C. 20503
(202) 395-5750
FAX (202) 395-3744

About the Authors

Steven J. Bennett is a full-time author who has written and/or collaborated on 45 books on topics including business and environment, entrepreneurship, business computing, and parenting. Among his other titles, he wrote *Ecopreneuring: The Complete Guide to Small Business Opportunities from the Environmental Revolution* (Wiley, 1991). Mr. Bennett holds a B.A. degree from the University of Rochester and an M.A. from Harvard University.

Richard Freierman is an environmental and business writer and consultant. A graduate of the College of Environmental Science and Forestry, State University of New York, Mr. Freierman gained field experience in forestry and wildlife research in South Carolina. His business and marketing background includes seven years as Product Engineering and Publications Manager for a manufacturer of medical imaging and process control systems. His other books include *Save the Earth at Work* and *Microcomputer Market Place 1993*.

Stephen George is an author and consultant with 17 years of experience providing communications and quality-related services to a wide range of business clients. His first book, *The Baldrige Quality System: The Do-It-Yourself Way to Transform Your Business* (Wiley, 1992), has been hailed by quality pioneer J.M. Juran as "the definitive book on the Baldrige Award."

Index